Publish
or
Perish

The Educator's Imperative

For all my special friends: Barbara, Carol, Dale, Laura, Louise, and Gwen

Publish
or
Perish
The Educator's Imperative

Strategics for
Writing Effectively
for Your Profession
and Your School

Allan A. Glatthorn

CORWIN PRESS, INC.
A Sage Publications Company
Thousand Oaks, California

For information:

Corwin Press, Inc.
A Sage Publications Company
2455 Teller Road
Thousand Oaks, California 91320
E-mail: order@corwinpress.com

Sage Publications Ltd.
6 Bonhill Street
London EC2A 4PU
United Kingdom

Sage Publications India Pvt. Ltd.
M-32 Market
Greater Kailash I
New Delhi 110 048 India

Printed in the United States of America

Library of Congress Cataloging-in-Publication Data

Glatthorn, Allan A., 1924-
  Publish or perish—the educator's imperative: Strategies for writing effectvely for your profession and your school / by Allan A. Glatthorn.
        p. cm.
Includes bibliographical references and index.
  ISBN 0-7619-7866-6 (cloth)
  ISBN 0-7619-7867-4 (pbk.)
  1. Authorship. 2. Authorship-Marketing. 3. Academic writing. 4. Scholarly publishing. I. Title.
  PN146 .G59 2002
  808'.02-dc21

                                                    2002000151

This book is printed on acid-free paper.

02 03 04 05 10 9 8 7 6 5 4 3 2 1

Acquisitions Editor:	Robb Clouse
Associate Editor:	Kylee Liegl
Editorial Assistant:	Erin Buchanan
Copy Editor:	Liann Lech
Production Editor:	Denise Santoyo
Typesetter:	Rebecca Evans
Indexer:	Kathy Paparchontis
Cover Designer:	Michael Dubowe

Contents

Preface

Why write a book about writing for educational leaders? For three reasons: because I think that experienced leaders have much to say to the profession; because I hope to reach those who are reluctant writers, having been there myself; and finally, because many leaders who have a story to tell just aren't sure how they should tell it.

Those reasons perhaps explain the special features of the book. First, you will note that the style is less formal. I know how to write the academic style (see Stuffy, 2003), but I wanted to speak to you directly. So, the only references you will see are those where I felt compelled to acknowledge my sources. And I hope that the style achieves its informality by my use of short sentences, colloquial expressions, and brief paragraphs.

Second, from time to time, I refer to my own experience as a writer, using the dreaded pronoun "I." Doing so was not an attempt at self-aggrandizement. Rather, it was a modest way to identify with writers who are still developing. I have known self-doubt as a writer. I have received numerous rejection letters. And I have made a bunch of mistakes, both major and minor ones.

Next, I make much use of figures, boxes, and exhibits in order to increase clarity. Let me define those terms briefly. A *figure* is a drawing, a sketch, or an illustration. A *box* (a term suggested by publisher Gracia Alkema) is a summary of key ideas and processes, set off from the regular text. And an *exhibit* is an extended example of a process or strategy.

Also, I have designed the book so that it may be used flexibly. If you would like some guidance, read the first nine chapters as they are sequenced here; then, select from the remaining chapters those you need most.

Finally, I make specific and direct recommendations about how to write the various kinds of messages because I know that developing writers want that kind of help. Yet at the same time, I encourage all readers to develop their own models and processes. In a sense, I hope I have achieved a balance of teacher-like directness and mentor-like support.

Acknowledgments

This work has benefited from the input of a few very special people. Many years ago, Sharon Schlegel was my student in Junior Honors English, and she suffered from my liberal use of the red pencil. Despite my criticism, she has become a very successful journalist. So, when I needed an expert for Chapter 18, I turned to Sharon. As usual, she delivered.

Dr. Sandy Petersen, staff development director for the Davis (Utah) school system, was foolish enough to offer to read the entire manuscript in progress. Her support was timely and her suggestions right on target.

Robb Clouse, acquisitions editor for Corwin, is, without a doubt, the best editor with whom I have ever worked. He has sure instincts for where the market is headed. He knows how to handle difficult authors who don't understand that he knows more about publishing than they do. And he is an expert in providing constructive criticism when that is needed.

About the Author

 **Allan A. Glatthorn** is Distinguished Research Professor Emeritus at East Carolina University in Greenville, North Carolina. He has taught writing for 25 of the 55 years he has been teaching. He has written more than 50 texts on the teaching of writing and more than 30 professional books. When he isn't writing, he is looking for dragonflies.

PART I

Getting Started

PART I

Getting Started

CHAPTER ONE

Becoming a Published Writing Professional

A re you, or do you wish to be, a published writing professional? Published writing professionals are professionals who write frequently about their professional knowledge and experience—and who publish what they have written.

THE REASONS FOR WRITING AND PUBLISHING

Why might you want to be a published writing professional?

- *To discover what you know.* Many writers attest to the importance of writing as a way of discovering and knowing. "I didn't know what I knew about ability grouping until I agreed to write an article about it."

- *To advance your career.* College professors know the reality of "publish or perish." Roman Catholic priests teaching at Catholic colleges give the adage their own twist: "publish or parish." Principals aspiring to the superintendency know that a list of publications in the resumé gives them an edge over unpublished colleagues. Published writing also calls attention to your abilities and increases your visibility.

- *To know the satisfaction that comes from making a difference in the lives of children and youth.* If children learn more by using a learning strategy that you have developed and published, you should feel a sense of gratification. The best educators are engaged in a life-long pursuit of meaning, and writing and publishing play a significant role in that quest.

  • *To become more effective in your present role.* By researching, writing, and publishing, you will gain skills and knowledge that should improve your performance.

Writing that is not published is like a tree that falls in the forest with no one there to hear.

THE DRAWBACKS OF WRITING

However, there are some crucial drawbacks. Writing takes time. You might spend as much as 20 full days writing and revising a brief article. You need to develop a tough skin. Your readers and editors will criticize your work. After writing some 30 books, I still wince when I get negative feedback. You put yourself on the line when you write for publication. Finally, writing is hard work, taking both a physical and an emotional toll. Such tasks as focusing on a topic, retrieving and evaluating information, and writing and revising a draft all create pressure and tension.

LEARNING TO WRITE

Published writing professionals strive to improve their writing throughout their careers. There is no magic formula that will transform your writing overnight; however, there are some simple steps you can take that will result in some gradual improvement.

Read Widely and Carefully

First, read as much as you can in professional journals. The reading process helps you internalize such skills as organizing the article and using research appropriately. The questions listed in Box 1.1 can help you focus your reading so that it results more directly in better writing.

Box 1.1   Reading to Write Better

The following questions can guide your reading when you read to write better.

1. *Audience.* Who seems to be the intended audience? What accommodations does the writer make for the audience?

2. *Organization.* What organizational pattern is used? Is the organization clear?

3. *Beginning.* How does the article begin? Is the beginning effective?

4. *Paragraph Length.* How many sentences in a typical paragraph? Is paragraph length appropriate for the audience?

5. *Word Choice.* Are technical terms explained clearly? Does the article avoid clichés and slogans? Is word choice appropriate for the audience?

6. *Documentation.* Are statements and arguments sufficiently documented? Are references current?

7. *Ending.* How does the article end? Is the ending effective?

8. *Article Length.* How long is the article in number of pages? Does the length seem appropriate for the audience?

OVERALL ASSESSMENT

By reading this article, what did you learn about writing that gets published? What suggestions would you make to the author to improve the article?

Write Frequently

Next, write as often as you can. Just the act of writing seems to make the writing go easier. Some writing professionals find it helpful to do some "free writing" when they hit writer's block. Free writing is simply writing whatever comes into your mind, without worrying about form, just to get the juices running. For example, here is some free writing by a writing professional who was trying to warm up for an article on accountability.

> Who's accountable. In any good school there should be account-ability on all sides. A balanced approach, emphasizing mutual accountability is needed, a circle of accountability. Students should not be left off the hook. They need to be held accountable.

Get Feedback

You will need to get two kinds of feedback. First, you will need a colleague who can give your article a close reading before you send it off. He or she should know how to find typos, such as misspelled words, misplaced commas, and sentence fragments; he or she also should be able to give you feedback about content. This person needs to be careful about details and have a good knowledge of English us-age and sentence structure. Skilled proofreaders use a standardized set of symbols. Figure 1.1 shows the most commonly used proof-reader's marks that you are expected to use in revising an article being prepared for publication. Keep the proofreader's marks near your word processor.

All writers (including me) also need feedback from the pub-lisher's editors; Chapter 9 provides you with more details about the several publisher editors with whom you might work once your writing has been accepted. These editors will give you feedback about such matters as writing style, audience sensitivity, and content accuracy. These are the kinds of comments a good editor might make:

- Seems out of place here

- Needs fuller development

- Add documentation

Figure 1.1.   Proofreader's Marks

INSTRUCTION	EXAMPLE	MARK IN MARGIN
delete	the sh̶y̶ boy	℘
insert	The ˄President	˄ *u.s.*
let it stand	s̶u̶b̶w̶a̶y̶ writers	s t e t
make capital	president	(cap)
make lower case	Autumn	(lc)
close up space	The chair man	c ! u
start paragraph	Too many educators	¶

These are the marks most commonly used by writers.

As is apparent from these examples, an editor deals with more substantive matters than a proofreader does.

Publish, Publish, Publish

As noted above, the ultimate goal is to publish. You get no points for manuscripts that lie on the shelf gathering dust. You make no impact on the profession when your good ideas have not seen the light of day. And you should not list on your resumé unpublished works, unless you include articles or books to be published in the near future, labeled as "in press."

The other major benefit is the contact with the professionals who serve the publisher on the editorial staff. I have learned a great deal from the experienced editors who have helped me improve my writing and deepen my knowledge of the publishing process.

Use This Book

The final process for improving your writing is to use this book intelligently. Although this book cannot, by itself, make you a good writer, it does present some experience-tested advice that should make improvement easier. The next section of this chapter explains how best to use the book.

THE ORGANIZATION OF THIS WORK

This book is written so that it might be used in a variety of ways. To help you use it effectively, you should know how the book is conceptualized and organized. As indicated in the table of contents, the book is organized into six main sections. Part I, "Getting Started," deals with preliminary matters in the opening chapters. This first chapter explains how to become a published writing professional, and Chapter 2 presents a process for finding a focus for your writing and making long-term plans. Chapter 3 explains how to use the tools of the trade.

Part II, "Mastering the Writing Processes," explains the essential skills involved in effective use of the writing processes, with one chapter for each process: finding a topic, building the knowledge base, organizing your writing, drafting with style, editing and revising, and working with editors and publishers.

Parts III, IV, and V explain several types of writing for three different audiences and settings. Part III is concerned with professional venues: professional writing for practitioners, articles for research journals, editorials and other opinion pieces, and writing your first book. The section concludes with a special chapter on publishing on the Internet. Part IV emphasizes three types of graduate academic writing. Part V will help you write effectively in the organization—publishing in the local paper and writing funding proposals. The book concludes with Part VI, which looks behind to summarize and ahead to anticipate.

The book is organized and written to give you maximum flexibility. You do not have to read the chapters in order. One approach would be to read the first nine chapters as a foundation and then select the type of writing most important to you, reading the appropriate chapter.

CHAPTER TWO

Focusing and Planning for the Long Term

Instead of moving aimlessly from article to article, you might find it useful to find a focus for your writing and develop a long-term plan for your writing career. The following process has worked well for many aspiring writers.

FINDING A FOCUS

Begin by finding a focus for your professional writing. Finding a focus is deciding in which area of your profession you will develop your expertise. Consider three different patterns of focusing.

1. *Pattern A: Limited and Multiple.* Pattern A is one followed by Anthony Armato, a school principal who, over the years, has pursued three areas of interest: curriculum development, learning styles, and brain-based learning. He reads widely, studying in depth these three areas that seem important to his school. In an interview, Anthony explains his position in this manner.

> As a principal, I think I need depth in a couple of areas that are most likely to help my school. But I don't have the time or the interest to chase after every fad that comes along.

2. *Pattern B: Single and Narrow.* Pattern B was used by Susan Markowitz, an assistant professor. Her dissertation was a study of gender differences in the self-esteem of fifth graders. Because she found that focus to be a very productive one, she has decided to pursue it in greater depth in her quest for tenure. As she does research in the field, her focus narrows, gaining depth in the process. She explained her choice in this manner.

> In the university you have to be a specialist if you want tenure. Once you get tenure and a full professorship, you can pretty much do what you want. But until then, make yourself a narrow specialist.

3. *Pattern C: Unfocused and Short Lived.* Pattern C was followed by Howard Washington, a high school teacher who has no particular interest in focusing. He has a bright, inquisitive mind, one that takes delight in following many brief paths. He jumps on whatever bandwagon is rolling by, chasing a topic while it seems "hot" and abandoning it as he loses interest. You should not see Pattern C as wholly negative. I followed Pattern C while I was a principal looking for good ideas.

Which of these is best? All three patterns of focusing can be productive. Whatever fits your own personality and career choice is a good pattern.

A Rationale for Finding a Focus

Although there is merit in each pattern, consider these advantages for focusing on a limited number of areas that you pursue in depth.

- *You can develop a strong knowledge base.* A scattershot approach leaves you with bits and pieces of knowledge.

- *You can write without having to do additional research, except to update your knowledge.* Good writing draws from a deep knowledge base, which is difficult to develop if you are juggling 8 or 10 topics.

- *You can develop a reputation in your area of expertise.* How would you respond if you were asked, "What's your area of expertise?"

- *You can consult in that area.* If others identify your name with a topic that interests them, then they are likely to invite you to consult: "Let's invite Creasman—he's really good on making schools safer."

- *You are more likely to find a publisher for your "big book" once you have established your reputation.* Publishers know the value of contracting with experts whose expertise is readily identified.

Determining the Focus

Consider several factors in finding your focus. First, reflect about your current interests. Because you will probably spend considerable time writing about the area chosen, it should be a topic that excites you. See if any of the topics generated by Box 2.1 stimulate your own thinking.

Next, consider the professional timeliness of the areas you are considering. There are obvious advantages in developing your expertise in an area that is just beginning to attract attention. Consider the implications of Figure 2.1, which graphically illustrates the rise and fall of educational innovations.

Reflect about a few examples. Outcomes Based Education (OBE) is moribund. The attacks of conservative critics and the ineptitude of its defenders killed what was essentially a sound reconstruction of the curriculum. Interest in Total Quality Education (TQE) has sharply declined since first introduced. The essential principles may last for a long time, but the movement seems to have petered out. My prediction is that classroom and home use of handheld wireless devices is ready to take off. Once their cost is reduced to $90 and their capabilities are increased, they will become the central means of acquiring information.

If these observations are sound, you would be foolish to choose either OBE or TQE as a focus. Instead, you should study the growing use of handheld wireless devices—or some other area that is about to

---

Box 2.1 Focus Finder

Directions: Consider all the areas listed below. Indicate for each the strength of your interest by using one of these numbers for each:

> 3: very strong interest
> 2: moderate interest
> 1: little or no interest

Learning   _____
Teaching   _____
School climate   _____
School culture   _____
Violence in the schools   _____
Curriculum   _____
Parent involvement   _____
Home schooling   _____
Charter schools   _____
Tests and assessments   _____
Special learners   _____
Technology   _____
Retention in grade   _____
Learning styles   _____
Brain-based learning   _____
Use of time in school   _____
Use of time outside of school   _____
School leadership   _____
School budgeting   _____
School transportation   _____

---

take off. But don't take my word for it; make your own analysis of what is in, what is out, and what is looming on the horizon.

Also consider the professional significance of your choices. A topic that has professional significance has not been overstudied and is considered important in your field. Consider this topic proposed by

Figure 2.1.   The Innovation Curve

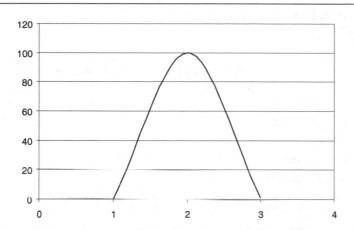

(but not accepted from) a doctoral student: "Is it less costly and time-consuming to change all the fluorescent bulbs at the same time or to change them only when they burn out?" That issue has some practical application, but it hardly counts as a scholarly question.

Finally, select a focus that will relate closely to and support your career plans. Consider these scenarios.

- George Williams is an assistant principal in a small rural school system. He aspires to the principalship. How should he determine his focus? One answer is to meet with the superintendent: "I will soon be starting my dissertation. Is there a topic I could study that would be of value to our schools?"

- Maria Gomez is just beginning her master's degree in chemical engineering. She wants to apprentice herself to Professor Alexander Marchut, renowned researcher in chemical engineering. Obviously, she will have to buy into his research agenda if she wants to work with him as a mentor.

- William Moses is a principal in a large urban district. He hopes he will be selected to join the faculty of a local teachers' college. He would be wise to do a dissertation in teacher education.

Alternative scenarios are possible, of course. The point is to choose a focus carefully to create a synergy, not fragmentation.

Box 2.2   Evaluating Topics

Topics	Personal Interest	Time-liness	Signifi-cance	Career Advance-ment	Total
Curriculum for special learners	3	4	4	4	15
Changing the school climate	3	2	3	3	11
Measuring the culture	2	2	2	2	8

Ratings: 1 = *weak*, 2 = *moderate*, 3 = *strong*, 4 = *very strong*.

Narrowing Your Choices

At this stage, if you are still unsure about your focus, you may find it useful to evaluate your tentative choices, using the criteria discussed earlier. Box 2.2 should be of help here. In identifying an area of concentration, use input from your colleagues, supervisors, and professors.

MAKING THE LONG-TERM PLAN

How can you juggle all your roles—parent, spouse, student, educator, scholar—and many others? One way is to develop a long-term plan, a plan that links all those disparate roles so that they support each other. As you read this section of the chapter, continue to examine Figure 2.2, which shows an example of a plan developed by Tanya Williams.

Develop the Matrix

Construct a chart similar to the one shown in Figure 2.2. Decide first how many years will be included in your plan. A 5-year plan

Figure 2.2.

Life Stream/Year	03	04	05	06	07
Career	Assistant Principal	Assistant principal	Principal	Principal	University professor
Writing	1 practitioner article	2 practitioner articles	Dissertation	Dissertation	Research article
Research			Research	Research	
Education	Finish course work	Take exams		Receive Ed.D.	
Personal				Marriage	Move

seems to work well. Then, decide how many "life streams" you will use. For example, you may decide to combine "personal" and "education." You also may wish to add a life stream, such as "church."

Complete the Career Life Stream

With the matrix in place, turn your attention to the career stream first. Tanya wants to be a university professor eventually. She is now in her first year as an assistant principal. She has heard that she will increase her employability if she has a principalship as part of her resumé. She decides to get another year's experience as an assistant principal before searching for a principalship.

Complete the Education Life Stream

Next, turn to the formal education life stream. Tanya knows that she has to have a doctorate for any university faculty position. Almost finished with her course work, she believes she can finish with one full year of residency and the rest on a part-time basis.

Complete the Writing Life Stream

Enter in the writing stream the kinds of writing you plan to do and the year for completing the writing. As an unpublished author, Tanya decides to start with an article for practitioners. She has worked successfully with an English/social studies team developing interdisciplinary units and believes it would make a good article. She decides to try to write two practitioner articles about extending her work on integrated units. She has heard that it will take 2 years to finish the dissertation. She also decides that she should try to get three research articles published in her first 2 years at the university if she is to earn tenure.

Complete the Research Life Stream

The next step is to complete the research stream. Tanya decides to use her dissertation research as the basis of her future research and publication.

A FINAL NOTE

How you plan is not so important as the quality of the plan. Develop a plan that gives your writing a focus and a purpose.

CHAPTER THREE

Using the Tools of the Writer's Craft

Every craft has its own tools, and writing is no exception. This chapter suggests which tools you need and how best to use them.

BOOKS AND JOURNALS

Some wag once touted a "new" technological aid: cordless, no complicated terminology, portable, inexpensive, flexible in use. The new aid, of course, is a book. The book is still so important that you should be sure to have your own writer's library.

A writer's basic library would include the following print resources:

- Two research journals that include research reports in your field

- One journal published chiefly for practitioners

- One college-level dictionary, with a copyright date not more than 5 years old

- A grammar handbook, for reference when you need to check punctuation or grammar

- A style manual widely used in your profession. A style manual gives you specific advice about such matters as formatting a table, using headings, and documenting references. Graduate students should check with their advisers for the recommended style manual.

- The classics in your discipline
- Major works in your area of specialization

A Writer's Notebook

You should also keep a writer's notebook. Its main use is to capture those brainstorms that come to you at odd hours. Because those ideas come at unpredictable times, you need a device that is completely portable, such as a small notebook or notepad. Here is a recent note from my writer's notebook.

all the euphemisms used about old age: if something ever happens to you . . . the golden years . . . senior citizens

You might consider buying a very small tape recorder that you can hold in one hand, recording brief notes while you commute or take long trips. Once you have captured those fleeting ideas in a small notebook, you can then enter the brief notes in an electronic journal.

Computer, Printer, and Word Processing Software

Although some writers cling to a pencil and yellow pad, most writers find the computer, the printer, and word processing software to be totally indispensable tools. Some special software tools are discussed below.

Grammar Checker

Word processing software also includes a style or grammar checker. A grammar checker advises you about writing style. For example, one rule in most grammar checkers is "Avoid using the passive."

That rule illustrates the value and limitations of grammar checkers. That rule is a useful general principle. Here is an example of where it would be helpful.

Poor use of passive: The book was read by the students.

Better use of active: The students read the book.

However, the passive is appropriate when the receiver of the action is more important than the doer. Here is an example of an effective passive.

Appropriate use of passive: The test was judged to be invalid.

The grammar checker found three "errors" in the first part of this chapter—all of which I rejected.

1. Use *wagged* instead of *wag. (Wagged* is a verb meaning "to wave back and forth.")

2. *Used* usually takes an object. (Not in my sentence.)

3. Avoid passive in *are discussed. (I discuss* calls too much attention to me.)

When the grammar checker suggests a change, test it in context. Does it sound better than your version? Does it convey more precisely the meaning you intend? Remember that the grammar checker only suggests; it does not mandate.

Spelling Checker

The spelling checker is such a useful tool that you should routinely use it after completing the first draft of every paper. Keep in mind, however, that the spelling checker will not catch such mistakes as using *to* for *too.* Box 3.1 is a list of frequently confused words that the spelling checker would miss if misused.

Box 3.1   Words That the Spell Check Would Miss

The sentences below show the correct use of words often confused; mistakes would not be caught by a spell checker.

1. I *accept* your apology.
   All may leave *except* Jones.

2. How did it *affect* you?
   What was the *effect*?

3. *It's* not too difficult.
   The school lost *its* accreditation.

4. *Whose* book is that?
   Who's on first?

5. *There* goes the car.
   Their books were destroyed.
   They're my friends.

OTHER USES OF THE TECHNOLOGY

In addition to the checkers just discussed, you will need the computer as an information retrieval tool, explained in the next chapter. The following uses are only some of the special ones available to writing professionals.

- *Establishing a Web or home page where you can tell others about your writing interests and receive messages from other writers.* A Web page is essential if you wish to make any commercial use of your writing. Each browser has its own process for setting up a Web page.

- *Receiving information from commercial e-mail.* If you do not mind receiving spam (Internet junk mail), you may wish to enroll in a shopping service that specializes in office supplies. One especially helpful is at http://www.shoppingplanet.com.

- *Discussing professional issues with colleagues.* A mailing list on the Internet is a discussion group that uses e-mail for discussing issues. A few Web sites keep track of mailing lists. One such list of lists can be found at http://www.neosoft.com.

- *Chatting.* You can join a chat room. The chat room is a place on the Internet where members can hold group conversations. Some writers find them a means of extending their contacts with other writers. Others consider them a waste of time.

- *Publishing.* If you are having trouble publishing in print journals, you have two viable options. You can publish your own writing, using desktop publishing. The Internet contains much useful information to assist you. The second option is to submit your writing to one or more of the electronic journals. The Jackson Library (Greensboro, North Carolina) maintains a comprehensive listing of more than 700 electronic journals.

OTHER HARDWARE

If you have ample funds, you may wish to consider other hardware you would use occasionally.

1. A fax for sending copies of selected pages to an editor or a coauthor.

2. A scanner for transferring print text to the computer. The scanner is useful for copying several pages from a book.

3. A copy machine for copying documents. For all copying, keep in mind the law as it relates to "fair use."

A FINAL NOTE

Although these tools can be very helpful, remember that they are only the means for facilitating your writing. They do not take the place of good thinking and writing.

PART II

Mastering the Writing Processes

CHAPTER FOUR

Finding a Topic

Most of the time you have no trouble finding a topic. Your boss tells you to prepare a funding proposal. You feel a burning need inside to write about a controversial issue. In such instances, the topic is obvious. In other cases, you have only a vague sense of what topic you should write about. This chapter should help you when this problem develops.

WRITE ABOUT WHAT YOU KNOW

"Write about what you know" is advice that successful writers most often give to beginners. You can write best about your experiential knowledge—what you have learned from your job and your relationships. Most experienced teachers could write about the following topics:

- When a lesson goes bad

- The first 10 minutes—the importance of a good beginning

- Good teaching without objectives

- Staying positive with disruptive students

- When parents don't show

Good articles of this sort require more than good writing. They first require you to be a sharp observer who knows which details are significant and how they are best recorded. Many writers keep a writer's journal for recording meaningful events. These articles also require insightful reflection, the ability to see beyond the obvious and find meaning in our lives.

STUDY PROFESSIONAL JOURNALS

Study the journals to which you hope to submit. This analysis is important because even an excellent article submitted to the wrong journal probably will not be accepted. Box 4.1 may be of use in systematically analyzing a journal. The main factors are identified, along with a brief comment about each.

USE THE FOCUS FINDER

You may remember from Chapter 2 that you identified several areas of strong interest. (See the "Focus Finder" in Chapter 2, Box 2.1.) Choose three that you would like to explore further. In the form shown in Figure 4.1, write in the three areas of interest. Then, systematically consider each aspect of the area of interest. The aspects are listed at the top of the figure. Where the area and aspect intersect, put an X, indicating a possible topic.

Here is an example of the process at work. Maria is the director of a new charter school, and she is interested in these three areas: teaching, charter schools, and curriculum. By examining the aspects, she is intrigued with the aspect of "problems." Then, she checks again the areas of interest, looking for another linkage. That process yielded this topic: "The problems of curriculum in charter schools."

GO AGAINST THE GRAIN

A good way to find a topic for an opinion piece is to "go against the grain," to challenge the conventional wisdom. Here is an example. At the time of this writing, there was a great deal of interest in "Brain-Based Learning," with some journals devoting an entire issue to the

Box 4.1   Journal Analysis

1. *Title of Journal.* Be sure to get it exactly right.

2. *Address for Submission.* Many journals maintain two offices; be sure to use the address of the editorial offices.

3. *Name and Address of Editor.* Many editors of scholarly journals maintain a university address.

4. *Style Manual Preferred.* This is an important detail, because using the wrong style makes more work for the editor.

5. *Refereed.* Most scholarly journals send articles to expert referees for their recommendations; such journals are called "refereed" and typically are accorded greater prestige.

6. *Query Letter.* Some editors prefer that you send them a letter describing the article and inquiring whether they are interested in the article.

7. *Acceptance Rate.* The reference librarian can direct you to a reference work that provides information about the percentage of articles accepted.

8. *Primary Audience.* The primary audience is the main readers for whom the journal is written.

9. *Secondary Audiences.* These are others who read the journal.

10. *Theme Issues.* Many journals announce in advance the theme for coming issues; for example, one journal recently announced that it wanted articles on school safety.

11. *Recent Themes.* If school safety was the theme for the most recent issue, it is unlikely that it will want similar articles for another year or so.

12. *Length Preferred.* Journals tend to be consistent in the length of articles they prefer; journals for scholars tend to be longer than those for practitioners.

Figure 4.1.   Area Focuser

Directions: List three areas of interest. Consider each aspect. Insert an X where an area and an aspect intersect. For each X, see if adding another area would lead you to a good topic. For example, you might list "differentiated instruction" as an area of interest and check these three aspects: history, problems, and successes.

Areas of Interest	History	Different Perspective	Funding	Problems	Success	Legal Aspects	Model Available	Philosophy	Major People	Factors	Personnel

subject. At such a time, one more article on the advantages of brain-based learning would not be very welcome. However, editors would be interested in an article questioning the validity of the entire movement.

Such a topic can be identified by "going against the grain," telling the bandwagon to stop for a while. Here is a simple process to use. Reflect about which programs and strategies seem to be faddish: They use slogans and catchy titles, are being exploited by several consultants, and are not generally supported by sound research. Check the research. *Research on Educational Innovations* (Ellis & Fouts, 1997) does an excellent job of presenting a balanced review of innovations such as whole language, learning styles, mastery learning, and cooperative learning. On the basis of your own experience and study, make up your own mind and write an article expressing what you have concluded.

FIND A PROBLEM

A very good source for topics is your own organization. All organizations have problems, and the research indicates that effective leaders are successful problem finders. (See Isaksen, Dorval, & Treffinger, 1994, which is an excellent compendium of problem-finding and problem-solving strategies.) An effective problem finder has the following characteristics.

1. Creates and sustains a culture where problem finding is encouraged

2. Welcomes teacher input, even when it is negative

3. Uses objective data to be sensitive to "messes," or situations suggesting that a problem is developing. For example, an increase in the number of students reported for disciplinary offenses may suggest an instructional problem.

4. Distinguishes among kinds of problems on several bases: importance to the organization; urgency or timeliness; number affected

Of course, problem finding can be too excessive. After serving for a year as acting dean in a major university, I created and posted in my office this message:

- All problems do not need to be solved.

- All problems that need solving do not have to be solved by Glatthorn.

- All solutions eventually become problems.

REFERENCES

Ellis, A. K., & Fouts, J. T. (1997). *Research on educational innovations* (2nd ed.). Larchmont, NY: Eye on Education.
Isaksen, S. G., Dorval, K. B., & Treffinger, D. J. (1994). *Creative approaches to problem solving*. Dubuque, IA: Kendall/Hunt.

CHAPTER FIVE

Building the Knowledge Base

B uilding the knowledge base can be considered the second step in the writing process. In writing memos and letters, you may spend only a few minutes on the knowledge base, as you call to mind the information you need. In writing a book or dissertation, you may spend a year or more. The more you know, the better you write. The more you write, the better you know.

Here is an example from my own experience of the importance of knowledge. If I decided to write a book on teacher supervision, I could probably finish the manuscript in 6 months. I have written three books on the subject and have extensive files. I would have to spend only a month to update my knowledge. On the other hand, if I were writing a book on school discipline, I would spend 5 or 6 months just building the knowledge base, because I have only a limited knowledge of the subject.

In effect, writing and knowing constitute a synergy—one informs and extends the other. Developing strength in one strengthens the other. The strategies explained below have been tested in practice and have been found to be effective. Modify them as you wish.

MAKE PREPARATIONS

Preparations are vital in building and using a sound knowledge base.

Distinguish Among Kinds of Knowledge

First, you need a map in your head of the kinds of knowledge you will encounter. Although it is not logically airtight, the following classification system works for most writers.

Opinion Pieces. This is knowledge about what someone believes, usually about a current controversial issue. The essential criteria for opinion pieces are the following:

- *Is the author highly qualified so that his or her opinions matter?* My opinions about school design are not worth much because I know so little about architecture. My opinions about curriculum do matter, I hope, because I have spent 40 years studying and writing about the school curriculum.

- *Does the author present a convincing case for his or her belief by providing reasons and evidence?* Simply stating an opinion is not sufficient. Readers expect to find opinions supported by carefully reasoned arguments and empirical evidence.

- *Does the author show an openness to other views of the issue?* Because there are at least three sides to every educational issue, readers give more credence to opinion pieces that recognize this complexity.

Here are some titles of opinion pieces that show the kinds of articles you might expect:

Teacher Leadership: Why We Need It

Merit Pay Is Without Merit

The Bright Side of Accountability

Reports of Practice. This is knowledge about how a practice, method, or system succeeded when put into practice in a particular organization. The criteria for reports of practical knowledge are the following:

- *Are readers provided with sufficient detail so that they may replicate the practice?* Replicating success is the chief reason leaders read reports of practice.

• *Does the report provide sufficient information about the results so that the practice may be evaluated?* Many reports of practice are much too vague about results, using statements such as this: "Teachers were very enthusiastic about the new phonics program."

• *Does the author explain the problems and difficulties experienced?* Because implementation problems occur with all innovations, they should be acknowledged and explained.

Here are some examples of titles of reports of practice:

Teacher Leadership—How We Do It in a Small High School

We Made Suspension Pay Off in Better Learning

Our Charter School Makes Standards Matter

Reports of Research. This is knowledge about the results of systematic study of some topic. Research is defined broadly here, encompassing a variety of quantitative methods (such as experimental, correlational, survey), and several qualitative types (such as case study and ethnography). Some research reports present knowledge in detail about one scientific study; some reports review the results of several studies. These are the criteria for judging research reports:

• Is the research question important enough to warrant study?

• Does the report explain how this study builds upon prior studies?

• Is the methodology explained clearly, and is it appropriate for the questions asked?

• Are the results presented objectively and discussed fully?

Here are some typical titles of a research report:

Teacher Leadership: A Review of the Literature

School Size and Leadership Dispersion

Designated Teacher Leaders: A Survey of Their Belief Systems

Theoretical Articles. This is knowledge of the assumptions, concepts, relationships, and axioms of some idea. Even though theory is often disparaged by practitioners, sound theory has several uses: It clarifies fuzzy concepts, it suggests key relationships and it makes useful predictions. You might use these criteria in judging theoretical pieces:

- Is the theory grounded in sound research?

- Is the theory clearly articulated, without excessive use of jargon?

- Does the article add significantly to professional knowledge?

Here are some titles that would suggest a theoretical article:

What Is *Teacher Leadership?*

What Is *Curriculum* in a Post-Modern Age?

A Conceptual Analysis of *Learning*

Indicate Your Priorities

Which kind of knowledge is most important? From my perspective, there is no absolute answer; the answer depends on the individual and his or her needs. Therefore, reflecting about your own priorities is useful as you begin your development of the knowledge base. Review your priorities in terms of the types you most need. That will change over time as your career goals shift. Here, for example, are the current priorities of George Phillips, a candidate for tenure who wants to publish in scholarly journals.

Topic: Charter schools

Top priority: Research reports

Second priority: Theoretical articles

Third priority: Reports of practice

Lowest priority: Opinion pieces

On the other hand, here are the priorities for Jeanette Rikers, an elementary school principal who is considering establishing a charter school.

Topic: Charter schools

Top priority: Reports of practice

Second priority: Research reports

Third priority: Opinion pieces

Lowest priority: Theoretical articles

This priority analysis should help organize the search process.

Prepare Your Files

In organizing your files, consider having two file drawers. You first need a general file drawer that simply keeps you up-to-date in your career field. Envision a file drawer or box with this label:

General File

A-Z

In that file are folders for each topic of general interest to you, filed alphabetically. Here are the first 10 files in my general education file.

Accountability

After school

Character education

Choice—schools of

College teaching

Community, school as

Constructivism

Cooperative learning

Curriculum

Grouping

Such a file has several uses. If kept current and reviewed from time to time, it can facilitate your work with colleagues. For example, you can speak knowledgeably with language teachers about new models of the language curriculum. It helps you distinguish band-wagons from significant trends. In retrospect, "whole language" now seems like a bandwagon; reading programs that use some whole language strategies along with structured phonics seem like a significant trend. It can also answer such parent questions as, "What is 'phonemic awareness'?" Thus, if you read an article of general professional significance, tear it out or photocopy it for filing.

The second file drawer is for your current writing/publishing interests. As this label indicates, this file drawer is for articles that seem important to you for your writing—according to your own priorities.

Charter School Curriculum

A-Z

Get to Know Your University Library

The final preparation step is to become familiar with the university library and its resources. Although you can retrieve most sources with your home computer, a good university library is indispensable for the serious writer. The library probably has some resources that you cannot locate with a computer, and they are likely to be very current. The library makes it easy to retrieve the full text of the source. And the library has personnel who can give you sound advice.

Use a Comprehensive Retrieval Process

With all these preparations made, you should now use a comprehensive retrieval process. Although several methods can be used, I have found that the one explained here is both effective and efficient.

Read Reviews of the Literature

Begin the search process by reading a review of the literature (sometimes called a research review). A literature review is an article by an expert in a particular field that summarizes the research in that area. Because such reviews are written at the invitation of the editor of a book or journal, you can feel certain that the author is a recognized authority in that area. The advantages of reading a review early in the search process are several: doing so provides you with an overview of that field, identifies the key issues, and notes the main authorities. You can easily find research reviews by including the term *research review* or *literature review* as one of the search terms.

Several sources usually include such reviews of a given field. Here are some useful sources in the broad field of education.

1. The journal *Review of Educational Research,* published quarterly, is devoted to such reviews.

2. *Review of Research in Education* is an annual volume that includes several review articles on two or three broad topics. For example, Volume 20 (Darling-Hammond, 1994) includes reviews of two broad topics: teaching, and equity issues. Each of these broad topics is divided into several chapters that review the research in special aspects of each broad topic.

3. Many separate volumes of research reviews have been published. For example, Macmillan has published very useful volumes in such areas as mathematics, multicultural education, and curriculum. These books typically use this phrase in their titles: *Handbook of Research in Teaching. . . .*

4. You can also use one of the databases in your profession to retrieve reviews by using the descriptor *literature review* or *research review.* The discussion below of ERIC explains how to use that education database; other professions have similar bases. (ERIC is an acronym for Educational Resources Information Center.)

When you find a good review, make a photocopy that you can mark and keep. Be sure that your copy contains full bibliographic information in the form required by your style manual. As you read, make a note of the key findings. If the article does not contain its own abstract or summary, write one that you can staple to the first page. Because this abstract is for your use only, you need not write it perfectly. Here is an example of an abstract.

Smylie, Mark A. (1994). Redesigning teacher's work: Connections to the classroom. In Linda Darling-Hammond (Ed.), *Review of research in education* (Vol. 20, pp. 129-177). Washington, DC: American Educational Research Association.

Summarizes classroom outcomes of the redesign of teachers' work. Examines career ladders, teacher leadership, participative decision making. Also considers in depth several classroom connections. An excellent review—needs updating.

Note a few features of the abstract. First, full bibliographic information is provided. Even though some style manuals use only the initial of the author's first name, note the full name in case you submit the article to a journal that uses the full first name. The abstract is brief, presenting only the highlights, and it concludes with a brief evaluation.

Retrieve Books in Your Area

Many students neglect to retrieve useful books. There is a relatively simple way to locate such books. Ask a reference librarian to direct you to the online or the print version of *Subject Guide to Books in Print*. This reference work is exactly what its name denotes. Organized by subject or topic, it provides bibliographic information about all the books on that subject currently in print. In using this reference work, remember that it does not include books that have gone out of print.

Retrieve Sources From Databases

Each profession maintains its own database that typically indexes all the literature in that field. For example, PsycLIT is a comprehen-

sive database for the field of psychology. ERIC is its education coun-
terpart. If you were writing an article on student motivation, you
should use both ERIC and PsycLIT. Because each database operates
somewhat differently, the following discussion explains a general
search strategy you can use with ERIC. For more detailed instructions
about a specific database, check with your reference librarian.

7.

1. Use the *Thesaurus of ERIC Descriptors* to identify the best
descriptors to use in searching ERIC. A *descriptor* is the term used to
search a database. Using the approved descriptor simplifies the search
process. If you have the time, you might wish to check the thesaurus
terms marked NT (narrower terms), RT (related terms), and BT
(broader terms). Suppose you decided to search the concept "school
climate." The online version would indicate that you could use
"school climate" or "educational environment."

2. Use the best descriptor to search the ERIC database. Let's
continue with the same example. You decide to search for references
to school climate. You go to the Internet and use this address: http://
www.askeric.org. You tell it to search for "school AND climate," for
references published after 1990, and for articles emphasizing research. Figure 5.1 is the first page of a three-page printout.

3. You next rate each bibliographic entry by checking the following: the title (is it on your topic?), the author (is the author an expert?),
the source (is it known for its quality?), the date of publication (is it
recent?), and priority compatibility (is it compatible with your priorities?). Use your own coding system for noting your ratings. Some
writers use a numeric rating, as follows: 1 = this reference is essential
for me; 2 = this reference might be useful for me; 3 = this is not worth
checking. Check my judgments to see if we differ.

4. Retrieve the abstract for each reference rated as 1 or 2. Figure
5.2 shows a typical abstract. By analyzing the abstracts, review the
ratings previously given.

5. Retrieve the full text for all those rated as 1. If you do not seem
to have enough articles, retrieve the 2s.

Figure 5.1.   Example of Initial Search Return

[Return to simple search screen] [Return to advanced search screen]

[Previous] [Next]

144 documents found (25 returned) for query : ((('school') AND ('climate') AND ('research')
AND (080) :publication_type) (AND (1990 OR 1991 OR 1992 OR 1993 OR 1994 OR 1995 OR
1996 OR 1997 OR 1998 OR 1999 OR 2000 OR 2001) :Publication_Date)

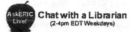 **Chat with a Librarian**
(2-4pm EDT Weekdays)

Score	Document Title
2 147	EJ511677. Dinham, Steve; And Others. School Climate and Leadership: Research into Three Secondary Schools. Journal of Educational Administration; v33 n4 p36-58 1995. 1995
3 144	EJ468667. Witcher, Ann E.. Assessing School Climate: An Important Step for Enhancing School Quality. NASSP Bulletin; v77 n554 p1-5 Sep 1993. 1993
2 141	EJ599683. Dellar, Graham B.. School Climate, School Improvement and Site-based Management. Learning Environments Research; v1 n3 p353-67 1998-99. 1999
1 139	EJ613025. McEvoy, Alan; Welker, Robert. Antisocial Behavior, Academic Failure, and School Climate: A Critical Review. Journal of Emotional and Behavioral Disorders; v8 n3 p130-40 Fall 2000. 2000
2 139	EJ543864. Slaughter-Defoe, Diana T., Carlson, Karen Glinert. Young African American and Latino Children in High-Poverty Urban Schools: How They Perceive School Climate. Journal of Negro Education; v65 n1 p60-70 Win 1996. 1996
3 138	EJ571161. Taylor, Dianne L.; Thompson, Bruce; Bogotch, Ira E.. A Typology of School Climate Reflecting Teacher Participation: A Q-Technique Study. Research in the Schools; v2 n2 p51-57 Fall 1995. 1995
2 137	EJ452853. Sweeney, James. School Climate: The Key to Excellence. NASSP Bulletin; v76 n547 p69-73 Nov 1992. 1992
2 137	EJ418125. Stevens, Michael P.. School Climate and Staff Development: Keys to School Reform. NASSP Bulletin; v74 n529 p66-70 Nov 1990. 1990
3 136	EJ517084. Thomson, William C.; Wendt, Janice C.. Contribution of Hardiness and School Climate to Alienation Experienced by Student Teachers. Journal of Educational Research; v88 n5 p269-74 May-Jun 1995. 1995
2 136	EJ480450. Kenworthy, Sue. The Moderating Effect of Psychological Characteristics upon the Visionary Leadership Behavior of Principals from Varying Levels of School Climate. 1994
1 136	EJ571159. Hardin, Dawn T.. Principal Leadership Style, Personality Type, and School Climate. Research in the Schools; v2 n2 p39-45 Fall 1995. 1995

CONTINUE TO UPDATE YOUR FILES

Keep your files up-to-date. Attend professional conferences, securing copies of papers. Write for papers presented at conference sessions you were not able to attend in person. Read current journals. Also

Figure 5.2.   Example of Abstract

OBTAIN

ERIC_NO: EJ599683
TITLE: *School Climate, School* Improvement and Site-based Management.
AUTHOR: Dellar, Graham B.
PUBLICATION_DATE: *1999*
JOURNAL_CITATION: Learning Environments *Research*; v1 n3 p353-67 1998-99
ABSTRACT: Examines the relationship between *school* organizational *climate* and the *school's* preparedness to undertake restructuring and improvement. Findings indicated the existence of an important relationship between organizational *climate* and the *school's* capacity to implement and sustain authentic site-based management. Where the *climate* is negative, tailored "front-end" strategies for improving the *climate* might be undertaken prior to the embarking on improvement initiatives. (AEF)
DESCRIPTORS: *Educational Administration; *Educational Development; *Educational Environment; *Educational Improvement; Elementary Secondary Education; *Improvement Programs; *Organizational *Climate*
PUBLICATION_TYPE: *080*; 143
CLEARINGHOUSE_NO: IR540725
ISSN: ISSN-1387-1579
LANGUAGE: English
ERIC_ISSUE: CIJJUL2000

OBTAIN

---

watch for new books by the experts. Every 3 or 4 years, clean out your files by discarding dated sources and those that no longer seem important. By using this process or your own version of it, you have established a general professional file that you can use to stay up-to-date and an organized knowledge base from which you can draw as you prepare to write and publish.

REFERENCE

Darling-Hammond, L. (Ed.). (1994). *Review of research in education* (Vol. 20). Washington, DC: Author: American Education Research Association.

Chapter Six

Organizing Your Writing

Writing that is organized clearly creates a better impression than does writing that is just a jumble of ideas. Well-organized writing is also easier to read and remember. Although you may have learned in high school that there is some "correct" way of organizing, the reality is otherwise. Any organization is acceptable so long as it is clear—and known by the reader.

This chapter accomplishes these objectives: It explains the nature and importance of reader-centered organization, describes several visual means for clarifying organizational patterns, explains how to analyze types of writing and audience, reminds you of the use of your knowledge base, explains how to make visual representations, and emphasizes the importance of making your organization clear to your readers.

THE NATURE OF READER-CENTERED ORGANIZATION

Effective writers use a *reader-centered organization,* regardless of the type of writing. As the term implies, it is a pattern of organization that attempts to order the sequence of content on the basis of what the reader wants to know. Exhibit 6.1 is an actual example (with all identifying information deleted) of a congratulatory letter wherein the principal failed to use a reader-centered organization.

Throughout this process of organizing, keep in mind two general principles. The first is that a clear written product is the payoff, not

41

Exhibit 6.1. Example of a Poorly Organized Letter

February 25, 200X

H.R. 209

Dear XXXXX,

The honor roll at XXXXX High School is divided into two parts, the first and second honor roll. The first honor roll, set at a marking period GPA of 3.8, recognizes an extremely high level of academic achievement. Within the first honor roll is a subset of students who achieve a 4.0 marking period GPA. I would like to personally acknowledge this subset of students because a perfect level of academic performance at this high school is truly quite extraordinary.

Students at XXXXX carry a demanding program of studies which includes five or six major courses plus fully graded minor courses and physical education. Earning straight A's in this environment is exceedingly hard. Those few students who accomplish this feat do so through a powerful combination of determination, effort and ability.

On behalf of the faculty and staff of XXXXX High School please accept my congratulations on your perfect performance during the second quarter. I know that we join you and your parents in taking pride in your achievement.
Please accept my best wishes for continued success.

Sincerely,

Principal

NOTE: All identifying information has been removed.

the planning strategy you use. Many writers do not make a written plan. They know their topic so well that they do only mental planning.

The second rule is that the audience is everything. As you write, continue to ask, "Am I reaching my audience?"

IDENTIFY TYPE OF WRITING
AND THE AUDIENCE

In addition to these general guidelines, you can do two initial analyses—of type of writing and audience.

Begin by Considering Types of Writing

Several different types are explained in Chapters 10 through 19. Each one has its own preferred organizational pattern. Besides checking those chapters for general guidelines, also study specific examples. For example, if you plan to submit to *Educational Leadership*, study the organizational patterns of the articles you find there.

This is the pattern you would probably find:

1. The problem the staff encountered

2. The solution they devised and the process used

3. The implementation of the solution

4. Their successes and the troubles that resulted

Consider the Audience

The following analysis identifies the major audiences to whom you will be writing and notes for each audience some factors that would influence your organizational pattern. Obviously, those comments are generalizations that do not apply to all members of a given group; they are only guidelines.

Practitioners. Practitioners (and more specifically, classroom teachers) want to know up front whether your article has any practical ideas for them. Most will want to know if there is any evidence supporting your project, but they do not want numerous references to "the research." Therefore, you might begin in this manner:

Every teacher has run into the special disciplinary problem of dealing with disrespectful students. For 2 years now, the Harper Middle School has developed its own approach to minimizing disrespect. The program has reduced by 20% the number of referrals for disrespect to teachers.

The authors would then explain briefly the process they used and the solution they developed. Next would come an identification of problems encountered and the successes achieved. Readers would expect the article to conclude with instructions for securing more information about the project.

Administrators. Administrators are concerned with organization-wide problems—funding, school security, community relations, principal's role in instructional leadership, and board-superintendent relationships. They want to read articles that reflect an understanding of those special problems and their roles in dealing with those problems. Here is how such an article might begin.

Every superintendent wants to be supportive of new ideas from the staff. In fact, most job interviews now include the question, "While you were superintendent at Lincoln, what new ideas did you institute?" Although such openness to new initiatives makes good sense, our school system has found that there are significant hidden costs with each new program.

Here is a simple outline for the rest of the article:

1. How we became aware of the problem

2. More details about hidden costs

3. How to handle ideas that are rejected

4. Specific directions about how other school systems might implement the program

Professors and Researchers. These individuals are accustomed to reading articles that begin with an abstract. However, some journals

do not use abstracts. Once you have written the abstract (if one is required), then try using an organizational pattern that follows the traditional research pattern: problem statement, review of the literature,
methodology, results, and summary and discussion.

REVIEW THE LITERATURE

Next, immerse yourself in the knowledge base you have developed.
As you read, note the major sections of the articles. Although you
may not use the same pattern, the review will remind you of the key
ideas.

MAKE VISUAL REPRESENTATIONS

At this stage, you should be able to make a visual representation of
your ideas. A visual representation is a diagram, sketch, or picture
that illustrates the main ideas. The research suggests clearly that such
representations have two advantages: They help the writer organize
his or her thoughts, and they help the reader comprehend the main
ideas and their relationships. Several visual devices are explained below. Try them to see which ones work best for you.

Conceptual Framework

A conceptual framework is a visual representation of the key
ideas and their relationships. Figure 6.1 shows one conceptual framework for the concept *effective school*. Conceptual frameworks are
most useful in discussing abstract concepts. You can make one in this
manner.

1. Identify the concept and its related subconcepts.

2. Draw a large circle in which you write the central concept.

3. Draw smaller circles and write one subconcept in each smaller
   circle.

4. Make a tentative sketch that shows the central concept.

Figure 6.1.   Conceptual Framework: Effective School

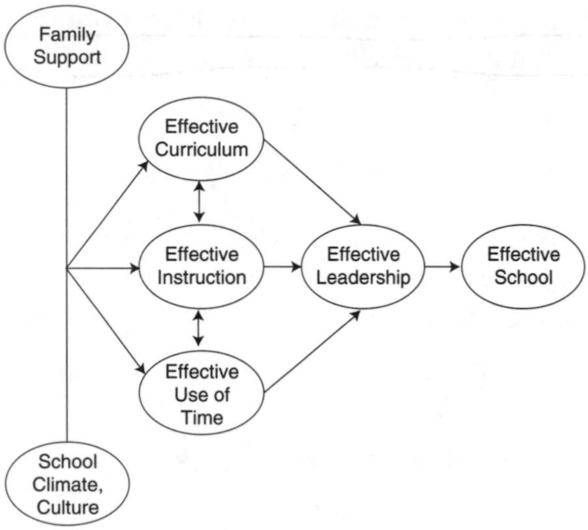

5. Place the subconcepts in a manner that shows their relationships to the central concept and each other.

6. As a means of checking the clarity of your sketch, ask a colleague to interpret the framework. Make any changes necessary.

Force Field Analysis

Use a force field analysis when you want to show the forces supporting and opposing change. Force field analysis is a helpful planning tool in assessing the forces that support change and those that oppose it. It is also helpful in delineating for others your analysis of the forces for and against change. Figure 6.2 shows an example of a force field analysis.

Try this process:

Figure 6.2. Force Field Analysis

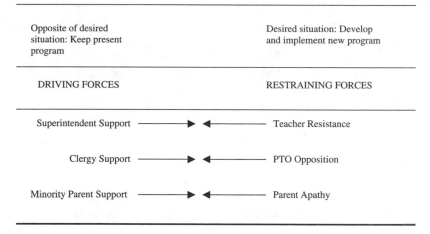

1. Prepare the form. Make a large T-shaped figure. On the horizontal line, note the "undesired situation"; in the middle, the "present status"; at the right, the "desired situation." The vertical line of the T represents equilibrium.

2. Enter the desired situation.

3. Enter the undesired situation.

4. Identify the driving forces, those forces supporting the change. List those with the arrows as indicated.

5. Identify the restraining forces. List them with arrows.

6. Have colleagues check the analysis for clarity and accuracy.

Flowcharts

A flowchart is a visual representation of the steps taken in a complex process. Flowcharts are very useful in picturing systematically what must occur in any project that includes multiple operations, such as developing a budget, building a school's master schedule, or equipping a new facility. Figure 6.3 shows the symbols commonly used in flowcharts.

Figure 6.3.   Flowchart Symbols

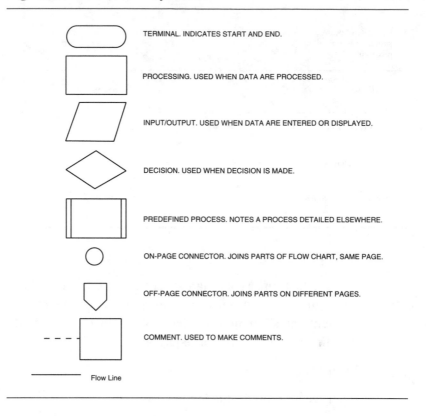

TERMINAL. INDICATES START AND END.

PROCESSING. USED WHEN DATA ARE PROCESSED.

INPUT/OUTPUT. USED WHEN DATA ARE ENTERED OR DISPLAYED.

DECISION. USED WHEN DECISION IS MADE.

PREDEFINED PROCESS. NOTES A PROCESS DETAILED ELSEWHERE.

ON-PAGE CONNECTOR. JOINS PARTS OF FLOW CHART, SAME PAGE.

OFF-PAGE CONNECTOR. JOINS PARTS ON DIFFERENT PAGES.

COMMENT. USED TO MAKE COMMENTS.

Flow Line

The steps in making a flowchart are simple enough:

1. Be sure a flowchart is needed. Use the flowchart for only major and complex processes. Do not make a complicated flowchart to show some relatively simple operation. For example, one of the books on Total Quality Management shows a flowchart for operating a copy machine, a relatively simple operation. Understanding the flowchart seems more difficult than operating the copy machine.

2. List the steps that seem important. At this stage, do not worry about details. Be sure the starting point and the goal are clear.

3. Use the standard symbols to translate the major steps into visual representations, using the symbols in Figure 6.3.

Figure 6.4. Example of Top-Down Flowchart: Unit Design

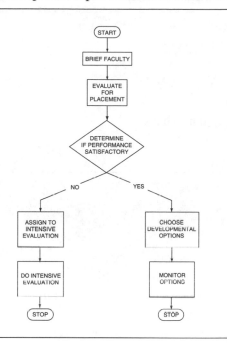

4. Add any details that seem needed for complete understanding.

5. Have someone relatively unfamiliar with the process interpret the flowchart, as a check for clarity and completeness.

Some experts suggest using a simpler "top-down" flowchart, which lists the major steps at the top of the page, in a horizontal row. Each major step is then analyzed into its specific actions, which are listed below the major step (see Scholtes, 1994). Figure 6.4 shows an example.

Outline

An outline is useful when you wish to emphasize the relationships of key ideas and their subpoints. Many writers dislike outlining because it brings back bad memories of 10th-grade English, when they had to outline their term papers. However, it is useful because it is so familiar. Figure 6.5 shows a simple outline.

Figure 6.5.   Example of Outline: English Curriculum

I. Language Study
   A. History of Language
      1. Early Languages
      2. English Language
         a. Grammar changes
         b. Vocabulary change
   B. Dialectology
II. Writing

NOTE: Only part of the outline is shown.

Idea Map

An idea map is a graphic showing in a free-form visual the main ideas and their related subconcepts. Figure 6.6 is an example of such a visual. Proceed as follows in making an idea map.

1. At the center of the page, draw a circle with the main concept written in the circle.

2. Show the first level of subconcepts by drawing circles of ellipses around the main concept, noting each subconcept.

3. Draw succeeding circles as needed for sub-subconcepts.

4. Connect the circles or ellipses with lines.

MAKE YOUR ORGANIZATION KNOWN TO YOUR READERS

Your final responsibility is to make your organization known to your readers. The following discusses ways of accomplishing this goal.

Use Headings Appropriately

Using headings is an easy and effective means for giving the reader the big picture. Because each publishing company has its own system for using headings, you should use that particular system. If

Figure 6.6.   Idea Map

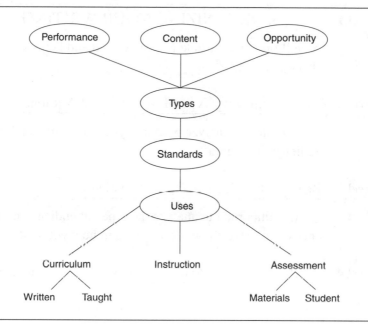

you are in doubt about which system to use, follow the guidelines of the *Publication Manual of the American Psychological Association,* 5th edition. Figure 6.7 shows the APA-recommended headings for a four-level article.

Provide an Overview

Notice the second paragraph of this chapter. It provides an overview of the chapter, helping the reader know what to expect. Although the overview is helpful, it can get tiresome if it is used too often or provides too much detail.

Use Topic Sentences

You can also use topic sentences to make the organization clear to the reader. A topic sentence states the main idea of the paragraph. Note that this paragraph begins with the topic sentence. Also, in paragraphs 3 and 4 of this chapter, the topic sentence comes first, its usual

Figure 6.7.   APA 4-Level Headings

Level 1	6. ORGANIZING YOUR WRITING

A well-organized article is easy to read and helps you check . . .

Level 2	<u>Identifying Type of Writing and Audience</u>

You should analyze both the types of writing and the audience for whom . . .

Level 3	<u>Begin by Considering Types of Audience</u>

It is important to analyze the types of audience preferences will make a major difference in how you write . . .

Level 4	<u>Practitioners as Audience.</u> Consider all the audiences . . .

position. However, the topic sentence can take other positions. Sometimes, the second sentence is the topic sentence. Sometimes, the last sentence is. And some shorter paragraphs do not include a topic sentence. However, research on text readability has established that using a topic sentence as the first sentence increases readability. If you find that the main idea of your longer paragraphs seems unclear, try adding topic sentences to increase organizational clarity.

REFERENCE

Scholtes, P. R. (1994). *The team handbook for educators*. Madison, WI: Joiner Associates.

CHAPTER SEVEN

Writing the First Draft

The drafting stage is different for each writer. The diversity partially contributes to the mystery of this creative process. Because there are no iron-clad rules, aspiring writers can only turn to the practices of successful writers. Following are some suggestions, derived from that knowledge base, for writing your first draft.

GET READY TO WRITE

Some preparations are helpful. First, develop a productive mind-set by believing in these affirmations, which many successful writers seem to hold.

- I can write clearly and effectively.

- All writing can profit from revision.

- Writing is a way of knowing. I will learn by writing.

- Reaching my audience is the priority goal.

- Writing is hard work—but the rewards are worth the pain.

Second, find a good time. Write when you feel fresh. If you are a morning person, set aside some morning time. If you are a night owl, find a quiet evening. Some writers need large blocks of time; others seem to be able to take advantage of shorter increments. One writer claims that she needs only 10-minute snatches of time to write something meaningful; I need about an hour.

Next, go to your writing desk, that place you have reserved only for writing. Clear the desk so that there are no distractions in the environment. Should you listen to music or watch television while you write? I vary in my practice. If I am writing material that I know well, I turn on the TV. If I am working on material that I do not know so well, I turn off the TV to concentrate. When in doubt, opt for quiet.

Assemble the knowledge base. If you have books or articles you plan to use, be sure they are ready to hand. If you are going to write about your experience, take time to reflect. Finally, develop a positive mind-set. Give yourself a pep talk: "This will be good stuff." We all have our low periods—usually caused by fatigue, depression, illness, rejection, and excessive self-criticism. Don't let yourself be defeated by those temporary aberrations.

How should you deal with writer's block? Write, write, and write. Force yourself to get some words down on paper, even though you know it's not your best work. I can assure you that you won't get back on your stride by complaining about writer's block.

LISTEN TO YOUR WRITING

As you write, be open to new ideas. Listen to what you are writing. Try reading aloud or to yourself what you have written. Writing is a way of knowing. Your writing will start to talk back to you, so capture what you hear. Do not be reluctant to start afresh if what you write is not your best.

BE AWARE OF PARAGRAPH LENGTH AND TOPIC SENTENCES AS YOU WRITE

As you write, be aware of two factors affecting your paragraphs—paragraph length and topic sentences. First, consider paragraph length. Although there is no "correct" length for a paragraph, as later chapters will show, some lengths are more appropriate than others. Appropriate length is determined by several factors: audience, page width, purpose, and medium. For straightforward prose that explains, many experts suggest that you write paragraphs that are six to eight lines long. When you see that a given paragraph is getting too long, determine if a shorter paragraph would look more inviting without damaging the clarity of the paragraph. Observe that this paragraph is *eleven* lines long (unless the editor breaks it up differently).

Also check on your use of topic sentences. As you may remember from English 101, a topic sentence states the main idea of the paragraph. The first sentence of this paragraph is a topic sentence. Research has determined that paragraphs (like this one) that begin with the topic sentence are easier to comprehend. Beginning each paragraph with a topic sentence is not an iron-clad rule, just a useful guideline for helping the reader.

INTEGRATE THE KNOWLEDGE BASE

The issue of how to integrate the knowledge base with the rest of the text needs special treatment. See if this method, used by many writers, works for you. The examples are based on the assumption that I am writing on the topic of differentiated supervision. If the article turns out well, I plan to submit it to *Educational Leadership,* read chiefly by classroom teachers and school administrators.

1. As noted above, I begin by mastering the knowledge base. I read through all the articles I have stored in the files in the study. I do not take notes but instead concentrate on internalizing the key ideas and relevant information, saturating my brain with this knowledge until I feel it is safely stored in memory. Because I have a comprehensive file on the topic and know the topic reasonably well, remembering the key ideas should not be a problem.

2. Next, I think through the organization I plan to use and the special method for showing the organization. I especially check my use of headings to be sure that they help the reader track the organization.

3. Every so often, I review what I have written, checking mainly for substance. Because I know that I have a tendency to reduce com-

---

Box 7.1 Diagnosing Your Drafting Problems

In your drafting, do you . . .

1. Develop a productive and positive
   mind-set?   ___ Yes   ___ No

2. Analyze your audience and the medium? ___ Yes   ___ No

3. Have in mind or on paper a good organi-
   zational plan?   ___ Yes   ___ No

4. Have a sufficient knowledge base?   ___ Yes   ___ No

5. Set aside sufficient time to get deeply
   into your topic?   ___ Yes   ___ No

6. Work at the same place for all your
   writing?   ___ Yes   ___ No

7. Think through an interesting beginning? ___ Yes   ___ No

8. Revise effectively and efficiently?   ___ Yes   ___ No

---

plex matters to simple lists, I examine closely the question of whether I have used too many lists. If I catch some misspellings in this review, I usually correct the error on the spot rather than rely on spell check.

    4. I read closely the succeeding drafts, usually writing three or four drafts until I am completely satisfied.

FOCUS ON RESULTS

Remember that there is no single best way to draft. If your present drafting techniques are producing good results, stick with them. If you are having problems during the drafting stage, use the diagnostic instrument shown in Box 7.1. Use the results to improve your own approach to drafting.

Chapter Eight

Revising and Editing

A ll formal writing needs both revising and editing. As the terms are used here, *revising* is making the big changes: adding content, eliminating verbiage, developing ideas more fully, and changing the organization. *Editing* is fixing up the small stuff: doing a spell check, using the thesaurus, changing punctuation, making sentences sound more mature.

KNOWING WHEN TO REVISE AND EDIT

Writers differ in when they revise and edit. Here are the options.

1. Many writers revise as they draft, and edit after the first draft has been completed. They write several sentences, thinking as they write, read what they have written, and then revise as necessary. After revising as they write, they then edit the piece.

2. Some writers revise and edit at the same time. They write a sentence or two, look back over what they have written, and revise and edit in the same time frame.

3. Some writers keep the two processes completely separate. They do a rough draft without worrying about form or content. When finished, they let the first draft "cook" for a day or two and then revise carefully. After revising, they do a quick editing to catch the worst mistakes.

Because there is no right way to handle revision and editing, you should find your own best process. The next sections suggest ways to make your revising and editing more effective.

GETTING HELP IN REVISING AND EDITING

Everyone (including me) needs a good editor and critic. You are so close to your own writing that you can't see the weaknesses and mistakes. Therefore, you need someone objective who can give you useful feedback. That process will be more fruitful if you clearly distinguish between three kinds of responses to your writing.

1. *Respond as Audience.* An audience is an appreciative reader/ listener. You invite an audience response in this manner:

> Do you think you might have time to read this letter to the editor? I just want to know if it hits the mark as you read it.

2. *Respond as Critic.* A critic is someone who responds with praise for the effective parts and negative remarks about the weak areas. You invite the critical remarks in this way:

> Could you please read this article for its big ideas? I'm going to fix up the mechanical errors, but I really could use some tough-minded criticism.

3. *Respond as Editor.* There are many kinds of editors, as you will learn in the next chapter. At this stage, you need a copy editor— someone who has good skills in spelling, word choice, punctuation, and sentence structure. Invite editing in this manner:

> Would you have the time to read this article before I send it off, just to see if I missed any errors?

You may wish to serve as a critic or editor for someone. Just be wary about providing those services for a friend or spouse. Being honest about someone else's writing is risky business. My experience is illustrative. At my wife's request, shortly after we were married, I foolishly agreed to criticize, edit, and correct one of her graduate course papers. I made it perfect, I was sure. A week later, the paper was returned to her, graded by a teaching assistant and filled with red ink corrections. What bothered me most of all was this bit of advice, scrawled across the top of the paper: "Get yourself a good editor!"

Regardless of who gives you feedback, professional ethics requires you to acknowledge his or her assistance. In a course paper, add a note like this one: "Ed Willis, graduate student, helped with the editing." If you are writing a book to be published, the help should be more formally acknowledged: "I wish to acknowledge the constructive assistance provided by Edward Willis, whose careful editing significantly improved the text."

REVISING EFFECTIVELY

The following discussion highlights the elements you should consider in revising. How you organize these processes is up to you.

Does the Writing Achieve Its Goals?

This first question is perhaps the most important. You should first consider your goals in writing this piece. What was your purpose in writing? Then read the piece as if you are the intended reader. Does it achieve the purposes you have for it? This is also a good time to reconsider any negative comments you have written. Remember that writing is more or less permanent.

Does the Piece Show an Awareness of Audience and Medium?

Read it again as if you are the intended reader. In these several aspects, does the piece clearly have the audience in mind in relation to the following: content, organization, research references, paragraph length, word choice? Suppose, for example, you are writing in a parents newsletter to explain how the school has changed. You use such jargon as *systemic, new paradigm, brain-based learning.* All the jargon confuses the parents, who criticize you for confusing them.

The medium is also important. Consider this example. The school has a new grading system, one that is somewhat complex. If you rely on the face-to-face medium, without supplementing your discussion with a handout, you have ignored the medium, because such communication is too fleeting for an uninformed audience.

Is the Content Accurate?

You must be sure that the content is accurate. Check all your facts and figures. If you include a direct quotation, be sure you have quoted the words exactly. If you paraphrase a source, be sure that you have not distorted the essential meaning. If you list a reference, be sure you have the spelling and punctuation correct. Several years ago, when I first began to write for publication, I misread one of the references and reported it incorrectly. I received an angry missive from the author of the piece I misread, who appropriately demanded that I correct the error.

Is the Tone of the Writing Appropriate for Audience and Purpose?

Tone in writing is analogous to tone of voice in speaking. Tone in writing is affected by word choice, sentence structure, and punctuation. Here are some various tones:

I deeply and sincerely appreciate the outstanding leadership you are providing us grateful followers—you are the greatest! (flattering)

We aim for perfection at Sommers High. And your speech to the students was perfect—perfectly awful. (sarcastic)

That speech was really bad! Next time, prepare better. We can't have disorganized presentations. (angry)

If you find that the writing has a negative tone, change it. Negativity in writing is almost always counterproductive. Here are some of the tones that will make you look bad:

- *Anger.* If you need to express your anger, do so in face-to-face communication. You can't take back angry words once they have been written.

- *Condescension.* People do not like being talked down to; show respect in all your writing.

- *Negative Criticism.* If some negative feedback seems necessary for someone else's growth, convey it in face-to-face communication.

- *Obsequiousness.* All people like to get positive messages, but do not make your praise too excessive or heavy-handed.

Is the Writing Free of Bias?

Media critics enjoy criticizing "politically correct" language— language that is excessively sensitive to potential bias. Yet a worse error is to use biased language. You have two sources of help here. The following list shows some common errors. In addition, Exhibit 8.1 shows one publisher's guidelines for authors.

- *Identify ethnic minorities by the term they wish to be used.* Many African Americans now prefer that term to "black."

- *Watch for the masculine singular pronoun—he, him, his, himself.* Using the masculine pronoun to stand for both males and females is considered sexist. Here are examples of the error and one way to correct the mistake.

Error	Correction
The pilot should check his instruments.	Pilots should check their instruments. (Change to plural to avoid the problem.)
A mechanic needs to buy his own tools.	A mechanic needs to buy his or her own tools. (Use his or her.)

- *Avoid stereotyping minorities.* A stereotype is based on the erroneous assumption that all members of a certain group have spe-

(text continues on page 74)

Exhibit 8.1   Author Guidelines

Author's Guide for Manuscript Submission

Preparing your manuscript according to these guidelines will help us make the production process a smooth one and keep the book on schedule. In the following pages, we have provided basic instructions for handling the various elements of your book, for preparing art, and for obtaining permissions. Instructions on formatting your manuscript can be found on pages 8-10.

Organizing Your Manuscript

A manuscript may contain the following:

- Title page
- Table of Contents
- Foreword
- Preface
- Introduction
- Acknowledgments
- Dedication
- Text
- Graphics: tables, figures, charts, graphics, photos, maps
- Notes
- References (works cited in text) with permissions as needed
- Suggested readings or Bibliography (works not cited in text)
- Appendix(es)
- Glossary
- Index
- Biographies of author(s)

Please begin your manuscript with a title page listing your full name, address, phone and fax numbers, and email addresses. At the top of each subsequent page, please type your name and the page number. Pages should be numbered sequentially from the beginning to the end of the entire manuscript. Please do not start each chapter with page 1.

(continued)

Exhibit 8.1   Author Guidelines (continued)

Double-space all material, including quotations, using one side only of white 8.5" by 11" paper. Allow sufficient margins on all sides; 1.5- or 2-inch margins are ideal.

As your contract indicates, we need two hard copies of your manuscript. Please do not staple, clip, or bind the manuscript.

TABLE OF CONTENTS

Please provide a detailed table of contents, listing not only chapters but also headings and subheadings within these chapters. We need this information to apply for a Library of Congress cataloguing listing for your book. This material will also be used in marketing.

FOREWORD

If someone else has written a foreword, either an introduction to or a commentary about your book, it should be placed immediately after the table of contents and before the preface. A contract will be needed between Corwin and the author of the foreword, so it is important to discuss any arrangements for a foreword with the acquisitions editor for your book prior to delivery of the final manuscript.

PREFACE OR INTRODUCTION

Sometimes the preface and the introduction are one and the same. If you have preliminary remarks about the volume, place them in a preface. The preface is an important selling tool and may contain a brief description of your goals, the intended audience, and distinctive features of the book. Detailed discussion of the purpose, intent, or scope of your work should be put in an introduction. Corwin follows the guidelines in *The Chicago Manual of Style,* 14th Edition, with respect to numbering of introductory material:

(continued)

Exhibit 8.1   Author Guidelines (continued)

A relatively short introduction that is relevant to but not part of the text itself should be paginated with the preliminaries, that is, with roman numerals. A long introduction or one that actually begins the subject matter of the text or that the author uses to set the scene—to give, for example, the historical background of the subject—should be part of the text, paginated with arabic numerals. (Section 1.52, p. 26)

ACKNOWLEDGMENTS

You may wish to mention people who have contributed to your research or helped you with writing and publication. Acknowledgments can be a public thank-you to those who have made a difference: associates, staff, family, students, editors, or others.

DEDICATION

A book's dedication is usually more personal than the acknowledgments. Here, you may choose to list parents, spouses, children, friends, or even entire groups of people to whom you wish to dedicate the book.

GRAPHICS

Place each table, figure, graph, or other illustration on a separate page. Number these to correspond with the in-text reference to the graphic, and group all the illustrations for each chapter together at the end of the chapter. Show the in-text placement of graphics by inserting a call-out in the text of the manuscript:

TABLE 1.1 ABOUT HERE

or

FIGURE 6.4 ABOUT HERE

Numbering Figures and Tables

Number figures and tables consecutively throughout each chapter. The first figure in Chapter 1 should be numbered Figure 1.1, the first figure in Chapter 2 should be 2.1, the second figure in

(continued)

Exhibit 8.1   Author Guidelines (continued)

Chapter 1 should be 1.2, and so forth. For example, the third table in the fourth chapter would be numbered Table 4.3. This numbering system allows the production staff to extract tables and figures from your manuscript for special typesetting codes while making sure that the correct graphics are placed where the call-outs indicate.

Preparation of Graphics

Keep in mind that we will reduce the art to fit within the type area of the page. Typefaces, too, will be reduced, and type smaller than 8-point type like this will become too small to read. Also avoid type that is unusually large and type that is too heavy—**TYPE LIKE THIS.**

Screens and shading do not reproduce well; please avoid using them. To distinguish sections in a pie chart or bars in a graph, use black, white, and black-and-white patterns such as diagonal lines and dots. We will need hard copies of all art. If possible, please provide electronic versions of the art as well.

Previously Published Art

If you choose to use artwork that has been previously published, we prefer that you send the original art. If you cannot do so, send the cleanest, sharpest copy possible. If the art was previously published in a Corwin book, we may or may not be able to retrieve the original for reproduction. Please check with us prior to sending your manuscript.

Any table or figure directly reproduced requires permission. Tables or figures that have been adapted probably will not require permission but are subject to evaluation by Corwin.

Note: "Adapted" means that you have added your own material to the original work to extend or expand an idea, and not merely "edited" down or rearranged the work.

(continued)

Exhibit 8.1 Author Guidelines (continued)

Remember that if you do not own the rights to this art, you must first secure written permission to reprint it. This permission must be included when you send us your manuscript. Please see the instructions on permissions for additional information.

Photographs

If photographs are part of your manuscript, please send them as black-and-white glossy or matte positives. Color photos and transparencies do not reproduce well in black and white. Please do not trim the photo. Do not use paper clips with photos; the clip can leave an indentation on the photo that may reproduce on the printed page.

Mark your photos on the back with a soft lead pencil, china-marking pencil, or soft felt-tip pen. A ballpoint pen or hard lead pencil may leave indentations. Avoid marking your photos or other art with Post-it notes that may come off.

Using a Professional Artist

You may choose to have a professional graphics designer prepare your art. Our acquisitions and production editors can recommend freelancers who do such work. Please share these instructions with any artist who will be preparing your work for Sage.

When preparing art for us to reproduce exactly as you submit it, please consult the detailed instructions for camera-ready art available from your acquisitions editor and on either the Sage Publications or Corwin Press Web sites. Detailed instructions for preparing and submitting camera-ready are also available from the Art Department at Sage Publications, the parent company of Corwin Press.

If you are the editor of a volume, please make sure that contributors have these instructions for preparing graphics.

(continued)

Exhibit 8.1   Author Guidelines (continued)

NOTES

If you use footnotes, collect them as endnotes and insert them at the end of each chapter.

REFERENCES

Thorough reference documentation provides readers with resources that enhance their understanding. If, within your text, you refer to a specific study or publication, be sure to provide complete bibliographic information in your reference section. The entry in the reference section should include author, title, date of publication, page numbers, and (for journals) volume number. Be sure to include issue numbers for journals that repaginate with each new issue. It is also desirable to include page ranges for chapters in edited books. Both in-text citations and reference listings must be consistently formatted. Corwin's preferred style is that of the American Psychological Association (APA), found in the *Publication Manual of the American Psychological Association* (4th edition). In this style, references are given in the text rather than in numbered notes, with the author's name and the year of the publication in parentheses. The proper format for the reference list itself can be found in Appendix 3-A on pages 189-234 of the *Manual.* The following are examples of APA reference list entries:

Journal article, two authors, journal paginated by issue:

Klimoski, R., & Palmer. S. (1993). The ADA and the hiring process in organizations. *Consulting Psychology Journal: Practice and Research, 45*(2), 10-36.

An entire book:

Cone, J. D., & Foster, S. L. (1993). *Dissertations and theses from start to finish: Psychology and related fields.* Washington, DC: American Psychological Association.

(continued)

Exhibit 8.1 Author Guidelines (continued)

Article or chapter in an edited book, three editors:

Callicut, J. W. (2000). Social and mental health. In J. Midgley, M. B. Tracy, & L. Livermore (Eds.), *The handbook of social policy* (pp. 257-276). Thousand Oaks, CA: Sage.

Electronic citations and references:

Information that you get from the Internet should be documented. For details, please see the APA Web site on electronic resources at

www.apa.org/journals/webref.html

or

www.uwm.edu/~xli/reference/apa.html

A number of Web sites offer general guidelines to APA style. Two good sources are

http://webster.commnet.edu/apa/apa_index.htm

and

http://www.uwsp.edu/acad/psych/apa4b.htm

PERMISSIONS

Copyright law is complex and extends protection to all media: books and publications, audio and video recordings, software programs, broadcast and news media, films, CD-ROMs, the Internet, and artistic or creative works, published or unpublished. As author, you shoulder the responsibility to obtain all necessary permissions and to pay any associated fees. Securing permissions can be a lengthy and expensive endeavor. How, then, do you know whether permission is required?

In determining "fair use," courts consider these four factors:

1. The purpose and character of the use, including whether such use is of a commercial nature or nonprofit educational purposes

(continued)

Exhibit 8.1 Author Guidelines (continued)

2. The nature of the copyrighted work
3. The amount and substantiality of the portion used in relation to the copyrighted work as a whole
4. The effect of the use on the potential market for or value of the copyrighted work

Corwin's general permissions policy is to require written permission from the original copyright holder to reprint or adapt the material listed here.

Artistic or Creative Works

Paintings, sculpture, fiction, logos, mastheads, and famous faces or body parts (models) require permission in all cases. Exceptions may be made when the work is the main topic with significant analysis. Permission fees for these works tend to be high.

Books

Permission is needed for the use of more than 500 cumulative words from any single full-length book. Fiction or poetry requires more careful consideration.

As with any other copyrightable material, it is Corwin's policy to require permission for use of Internet or Web materials unless a particular use can be qualified as fair use or public domain.

Interviews

Whenever possible, obtain a release to publish. If you cannot secure a release, depending on the nature of the interview and whether you identify the participants, we may need to exclude or otherwise protect the identities of individuals or entities.

Journal Articles or Anthology Chapters

Use of more than 300 cumulative words from any single journal article or chapter requires permission. If your book includes

(continued)

Exhibit 8.1 Author Guidelines (continued)

entire articles or chapters already published elsewhere, permission must be granted by the original copyright holder. Because it is frequently a condition that the chapter appear as it was published and not be altered in any way, your permission request should specify whether you intend to edit the work.

Newspapers or Magazines

Permission is needed for the use of more than two or three sentences. Authors must couple this use with analysis. If you intend to use mastheads, photos within articles, captions, or logos, you must spell these out on your request for permission, as these rights may be held separately.

Photos

In addition to permission from the copyright holder, if the photo was taken in a private location or is of a professional model, its use may require the subject's signed release. Photos of minors require releases from the minors' parents or guardians.

Poetry or Lyrics

Anything, even a few words or a phrase and especially when used for effect rather than analysis, requires permission. These fees tend to be high.

Speeches

Unless the speech is a political or campaign speech, its use probably requires permission if it is fixed in a tangible form (written or recorded).

Permissions Procedure

Please send permissions to Corwin along with your manuscript, keep a copy for your records, and include the corresponding chapter or manuscript page numbers. Upon request, Corwin can

(continued)

Exhibit 8.1   Author Guidelines (continued)

provide you with more detailed information on what requires permission and how to obtain it, and we can supply you with the necessary forms. A copy of the standard request for permission is included at the end of this guide.

GLOSSARY

If you use terms that are likely to be unfamiliar to your readers, you may find it unwieldy to define these terms within the text itself. A glossary offers the opportunity to provide a separate section of terms and their definitions. This feature may also set your book apart from the competition.

INDEX

Indexing your book usually increases its value to readers. If your book is to be indexed, your publishing contract will specify whether you are responsible for preparing the index or whether Corwin will have it prepared by a professional indexer. The contract will also indicate whether you or Corwin is responsible for the cost of professional indexing.

Regardless of who prepares the index, you can facilitate the process by developing a list of key words that should appear in the index. Further information on index preparation is provided in a booklet of indexing instructions for Corwin authors available from your acquisitions or production editor.

BIOGRAPHICAL SKETCH

Along with your manuscript, please send us a brief biographical sketch of about 250 words. The sketch should begin with your current position and may contain titles, affiliations, the focus of professional pursuits, and other information you wish to share with your readers. For edited volumes, biographical information will also be needed for the contributors. Normally, the editor's bio will be 100 to 150 words and the contributor bios about

(continued)

Exhibit 8.1 Author Guidelines (continued)

75 to 100 words. Corwin does not include information about undergraduate degrees. If you include information about postgraduate degrees, please include it for all contributors.

CONTACT INFORMATION

If you are the editor or lead author of a volume, please provide a detailed list of all contributors and authors. Include their full names (with middle initials or middle names if these are to appear in the book), complete street addresses, telephone and fax numbers, and email addresses. Because Corwin sends the typeset contributor proofs electronically (as PDF files), it is crucial to provide email contact information.

If you or any contributors will have alternate or temporary addresses during the text 10 months, please list these as well. Throughout the production of your book, staff will depend on this list to link them to the people who can answer questions or provide clarification. Without this crucial information, production can be significantly delayed.

Formatting Your Manuscript

After your manuscript is transmitted to the production department at Sage, both a disk and hard copy will be given to the copy editor, who will check the accuracy of cites and references, read for sense, make corrections in spelling, punctuation, and grammar, and insert coding necessary for typesetting. In preparing the text files, keep in mind that for production purposes, a simple presentation is best. A few basic formatting features (bold, italics, capitalization) should be used to make clear what level each heading is, what material is quoted directly from another source, and where graphics and other special material (such as boxed text) should be placed. Using additional formatting features to enhance the presentation may actually hinder production.

(continued)

Exhibit 8.1   Author Guidelines (continued)

HEADS AND LISTS

The heading for this whole section, "Formatting Your Manuscript," is a main heading or Level 1 head. These should be centered and can be set in bold type. The head above the beginning of this paragraph, "Heads and Lists," is a Level 2 head and should be set in all caps, flush left.

Subordinate Heads

The heading above this paragraph, "Subordinate Heads," is a Level 3 head and is set with initial caps, flush left. A fourth head level is one that is run into the text like the heads below that discuss different types of lists ("Numbered Lists" and "Bulleted Lists"). They are normally italicized. Each word may be capped if the head is short; if it is a complete sentence or is very long, only the first word is usually capitalized.

Two Kinds of Lists

Numbered Lists. Use numbered lists to present information that is sequential. In APA style, however, present elements in a series within a paragraph or sentence with lowercase letters in parentheses:

The participant's three choices were (a) working with one other participant, (b) working with a team, and (c) working alone.

Bulleted Lists. Use bulleted lists with care. The bullets call attention to each item in the list and can be visually useful in breaking up text. It's important not to overdo the use of bullets, however; the text itself should always be more important than the numbers or bullets you use to organize material.

EXTRACTS

The copy editor will determine whether direct quotations, or extracts, should be set as regular body text or indented and set as

(continued)

Exhibit 8.1   Author Guidelines (continued)

---

an extract. The general guideline is that quotations of 40 words or more should be indented. When your book is typeset, long extracts will be set single-spaced and may also be in somewhat smaller type than regular text. In preparing your manuscript, you may want to indent long quotations; however, please double-space all material, including extracts of any length.

COMPUTER DISKS

Our production staff can work with most word-processing programs, although we prefer that you submit your manuscript on disks in Microsoft Word or WordPerfect. In creating your files, please follow these guidelines:

Place each chapter in a separate file.

Make sure that the hard copy of your manuscript matches the files on disk. If you are the editor of a volume, make sure that the hard copy of the chapters you submit matches the disk supplied by the contributor or by you. Production can be seriously delayed if there are questions concerning what constitutes the final version of the chapter.

Label your disk(s) with the following:

1. Your name and, if different, the lead author's name
2. The name of the book
3. The name and version of the program you are using (e.g., MS Word 6.0 for Windows)
4. The names of the files on the disk

---

cial talents or characteristics. Can you identify the stereotyping in this example?

> Women talk about their feelings too much. Men do not seem so feeling oriented.

Is the Organization Clear to the Reader?

As explained in Chapter 6, you should develop and use an organizational strategy that will make sense of the content. In the revising process, you should be chiefly concerned with whether the organization is clear to the reader. As you revise, keep in mind the most important strategies explained in Chapter 6. The following strategies should be helpful.

Use headings in longer pieces. The use of headings can help the reader track the organization. Consider the use of headings in this chapter. By skimming the headings, you should be able to see that the chapter has these major divisions: knowing when to revise and edit, getting help in revising and editing, knowing what to revise, and editing for correctness and effectiveness.

Most writers create headings as they write, being sure that the headings match the organization of the piece. You should also check with the publisher about heading style, because there is some variation here.

Provide an overview in the opening paragraph. In longer pieces, you may wish to write a sentence in the first paragraph that provides an overview of the piece. Here is an example:

> There is currently a great deal of interest in the concept of accountability. Yet the term is used very loosely. This article will define the concept, analyze deficiencies in the present use of the term, and present an alternative conceptualization.

The last sentence in the paragraph tells the reader specifically what to expect.

Use topic sentences in longer explanations. As explained previously, the topic sentence is the key sentence of the paragraph, one that states the paragraph's main idea. Many writers do not use topic sentences consciously, but the research indicates clearly that the use of topic sentences increases reader comprehension. Consider the following two paragraphs to note the difference.

1. The first element in increasing student motivation is helping learners set meaningful and achievable goals. The use of such goals seems to enhance that inner drive to achieve. It is also important to help the learner believe in his or her ability to achieve that goal. Holding high expectations for one's performance is essential. Finally, teachers can emphasize intrinsic rewards, chiefly the satisfaction of learning.

2. Teachers can take several steps to increase students' motivation to learn. The first element in increasing student motivation is helping learners set meaningful and achievable goals. The use of such goals seems to enhance that inner drive to achieve. It is also important to help the learner believe in his or her ability to achieve that goal. Holding high expectations for one's performance is essential. Finally, teachers can emphasize intrinsic rewards, chiefly the satisfaction of learning.

The underlined topic sentence in Paragraph 2 makes it easier for the reader to grasp the central idea of the paragraph.

EDITING CAREFULLY

In editing, you should "sweat the small stuff," to paraphrase the title of the book popular in the 1990s. Although a misplaced comma may not seem important by itself, careful editing makes a positive impression and keeps the reader's attention on content, not form. The following discussion will help you use an effective process and avoid the most common errors.

A Recommended Process

You can edit any way that works for you. The following process has worked well for many writers.

1. Begin by editing on the screen—editing as you go.

2. Use the spell checker to catch obvious errors.

3. Use the thesaurus to check the need for word variety.

4. Use the grammar or style checker to note any major changes needed.

5. Print a hard copy.

6. Check it carefully for words omitted.

7. Strike out any unnecessary words.

8. Have your editor read the hard copy to catch any other errors.

9. In your notebook, list any errors that were due to your ignorance, not to missed keystrokes or carelessness.

10. Check any writer's handbook to be alerted to errors frequently made by some writers.

11. Make a special check of references.

This last point about references requires some special analysis. Novice writers often become careless in the way they handle references. Here are some common mistakes: forgetting to include in the reference list a citation noted in the text, forgetting to include in the text a source included in the reference list, spelling the author's name wrong, having one date in the text and another one in the reference list for the same source, and using the wrong format in the reference list.

Here is one effective method for checking for exact correspondence between text sources and reference list.

• As you edit on a hard copy of the chapter, look closely for the citations in the text. As you find a source in the text, examine the reference list.

• Make a check mark in the reference list for all references found in the text.

• Add to the reference list any sources included in the text and omitted in the reference list.

• Add to the text any citations noted in the reference list but missed in the text—or delete those references from the reference list.

Learn From Your Recurring Mistakes

You should understand and correct your own repeated mistakes. The most common mistakes made by professionals are explained below. Keep a list of these recurring errors near your writing station. Check the list from time to time, as you draft, to keep the list up-to-date.

Avoid the Colloquial Style in Formal Pieces

A colloquial style is one that sounds like conversation. Although it is effective in informal writing, it is inappropriate in formal communication. It presumes a closer relationship than actually exists. Here is an example of an inappropriate colloquial style in a letter to parents.

> Dear folks,
>   I wanted to brag on our honor roll students. Your youngster is included in that distinguished group. You know that we have tough standards; we're not in the business of passing out the A's. And these honor roll kids are not grade-grinds. They all are active. In sports. Playing in the band. Studying nature in the science club. You folks know how busy your kids are.

As that example indicates, several elements are involved in the colloquial style: short, simple sentences; sentence fragments; and word choice. Of these three, word choice has the strongest influence. Frequently used colloquialisms are explained in most handbooks.

Write Mature Sentences

The simplest advice here is to watch for "and" and "but." Here are some examples of immature sentences that result from the misuse or excessive use of "and" and "but."

1. Our difficulty in recruiting teachers was a result of offering low salaries, and the remoteness of the school was also a factor.

2. The football team requires a substantial budget, but it also enjoys the strongest community support.

3. The teachers are striking over accountability, and they are also unhappy about their working conditions.

The problem with "and" and "but" is that they are coordinating conjunctions that are used to indicate that two elements are equal. In actuality, one element is more important than the other. This unequal relationship should be suggested by using joining words such as "when," "while," "since," or "although." Notice how the sentences below suggest a more mature style than those above.

1. Our difficulty in recruiting teachers results from low salaries and school remoteness.

2. Although the football team requires a substantial budget, it also enjoys the strongest community support.

3. The teachers are striking over accountability and working conditions.

Avoid the Excessive Use of Jargon

Jargon is the technical language of an occupation. Here are some examples of educator jargon: high stakes tests, performance assessment, standards, curriculum coordination. Although this special language simplifies communication between educators, keep in mind two cautions. First, in speaking or writing with other educators, avoid educational jargon that has been overused. Here is a school principal writing about the need for change, using too much jargon.

There is a need for a new paradigm in educational change. This new paradigm will emphasize systemic change in the learning organization. In that learning organization, all children will learn.

Those few sentences are so filled with worn-out jargon that they contain very little substance, even for other educators.

The second reminder is to especially avoid all educational jargon in communicating with parents. How would you rewrite this teacher's letter to parents?

Sally is experiencing some difficulty in her interactions with age-mates. She seems to be having counterproductive experiences in defining and accepting boundaries to the extent that she frequently manifests antisocial behaviors. In her academic work, she also is having difficulty in our new Direct Instruction model. Consonant blends frequently cause problems.

Here is one rewritten version:

Sally sometimes has problems with other students. At times, she gets too close; at other times, she gets into conflict with them. She also has some difficulties in reading, especially sounds like the *pl* in *please.*

CHAPTER NINE

Publishing: Working With Editors and Publishers

The last—and in many ways, the most important—step in the writing process is getting published. "Getting published" is used broadly here to encompass several ways of bringing your writing to the attention of others—from reading your article to a circle of friends to having a major publishing house publish your book. This chapter takes you step by step through the publishing process, giving primary attention to book publishing. The last section of the chapter explains the special opportunity of publishing in journals.

CHOOSING THE RIGHT VENUE

You have a story to tell, and, like the Ancient Mariner, you should tell it to anyone who will listen. The first thing you should do is select the right venue for your book or article. You have several options here.

Writers' Circle

One easy way to get feedback is to organize or join a circle of writers that will meet to read manuscripts in the developmental stage. A writer who has benefited from such groups offers these practical suggestions for readers and responders (Van Ryder, 1992):

For Readers

- Do not apologize for your writing being too rough; if it is too rough, it's not ready to read.

- It may be useful to indicate purpose and audience.

- Never apologize for being a poor writer; the group will realize that soon enough.

- Read slowly. If you will take more than the allotted 15 minutes, read only part. Read poetry even more slowly.

- Don't offer side comments; let the writing speak for itself.

For Responders

- Talk first on what works. Discuss the major aspects—tone, clarity, pace.

- Note minor grammatical errors on a piece of paper that you can give to the reader.

- Don't repeat points someone else has made.

- Don't criticize content; keep your focus on the writing.

- Don't give the reader excessive praise; it doesn't help.

- Don't ask many questions; you will likely receive more information than you want.

The writers' circle has several advantages for unpublished writers especially. It provides a receptive audience. It can give you feedback for a work in progress. It can give you an ear to the grapevine about who is looking for articles and books. And it can give you support when the dark days come. The main drawback is the time it takes. As one task-oriented writer put it, "No circle for me—I'd rather be writing." If the idea of getting feedback appeals to you but the social aspects deter you, consider joining a chat group on the Internet.

Presenting a Paper

A good way for beginning writers to get noticed is to present a paper at a professional conference—either regional or national. You would have a good chance if you sent a paper to the program committee of a regional conference, because there is less competition than at the national level. And a good paper can be published as part of the conference proceedings or revised for submission to a journal. Here is a tip from a veteran presenter: Write the paper and then deliver it without reading it. Listening to a paper being read is a very boring experience.

Self-Publishing

You can be your own publisher, taking over most of the functions of the publisher: acquiring, editing, designing, contracting with a printer and binder, proofreading, promoting, and delivering. In doing so, you will be joining some distinguished predecessors. Mark Twain and Walt Whitman self-published some of their own best work. And the tradition flourishes to this day. The *New York Times* (Tabor, 2000) carried an article about Benjamin Kaplan, a 23-year-old author who self-published his book *How to Go to College for Free: The Secrets of Winning Scholarship Money.* At the time the article appeared, Kaplan had sold 25,000 copies of the book.

A very helpful resource for those brave enough to self-publish is Ross and Ross's (1994) *The Complete Guide to Self-Publishing.* With sophisticated publishing technology available, give serious consideration to self-publishing.

Self-publishing has some clear advantages. The author gets all the profits, not a small percentage. There are no editors to please. And the author makes all the decisions. However, there are also some drawbacks. There is no feedback process. The author often feels consumed by all the details of book production. And there is a great risk of significant monetary loss. I speak here with some unpleasant memories. Many years ago, I self-published a satiric poster about summer guests. My plan was to sell 1,000 copies for $1.00 per copy to gift shops in the Adirondacks, who in turn could sell them for $3.00. Does anyone want to buy 975 posters about summer guests?

Vanity Press

A vanity press is a company that will print the book by charging the author for all costs. It is called a vanity press because it appeals to the vanity of unpublished authors. The vanity press charges the author an up-front fee ($5,000-$20,000) to cover all its expenses in publishing the book and making a profit.

Here is how the vanity press operates. The press places a small ad in writers' magazines soliciting manuscripts. The unpublished writer mails off a manuscript that has already been rejected several times by commercial publishers. The writer receives a quick response: "You have a winner here! We'd like to work with you in polishing and publishing the manuscript." The press explains the services they will provide—editing, printing, promoting, and marketing. Of course authors need these vital services to bring this marvelous book to a waiting world. In fine print, the vanity press asks for a credit card number or a check for the up-front fee.

The vanity publisher then provides the promised services in a minimal way: A quick editing is done, a small quantity of books is printed and placed in cooperating bookstores, and a small ad is placed in a struggling magazine. The author and family are the only ones who buy the book. The author has lost a significant sum of money. Here's a good rule of thumb: Do not deal with anyone who wants to charge you for publishing your book. The publisher should be paying you, not charging.

Commercial Publishing

The commercial publisher is the best venue. Like all corporations, publishers are concerned with the bottom line. However, at the same time, they wish to be seen as a quality house that produces quality books. From the author's perspective, they provide useful services. The commercial house provides constructive editing. Their designer develops an attractive design. The best ones market your book effectively. And they pay you royalties for all the books sold.

The only drawback I have discovered is that most commercial publishers are very market sensitive. As a consequence, they usually play it safe, rejecting content that might be controversial. Many years ago, I received a phone call from an editor who had helped me develop a secondary English text. "I have good news—we were adopted in Texas, but you'll have to make several changes." I asked for examples. "You frequently ask kids to write about their families—that's a no-no in Texas."

If you have a choice, go for the commercial publisher.

Electronic Publishing

Are you interested in electronic publishing? This venue is changing almost daily and expanding rapidly, to the extent that you need to use the Internet to track current developments in e-publishing. A full discussion of electronic publishing can be found in Chapter 14.

CHOOSING A PUBLISHER

Once you have chosen a venue, you should choose a specific publisher, which is a complex and critical process. Let's assume you have chosen commercial publishing as the venue. What process should you follow?

Identifying the Criteria

Begin by identifying your criteria. Consider the following:

1. Is the publisher legitimate? Beware of the vanity press. In general, stick with the commercial houses. If you are tempted to play the vanity game, remember that a legitimate publisher will pay you, instead of asking you to pay the publisher.

2. What books has the publisher already published in your area of interest? If the publisher already has several successful books in your area, the acquisitions editor is probably not interested in one more. On the other hand, avoid publishers who have no books in your area. Your best opportunity will be with a publisher interested in expanding the company's line.

3. Does the publisher have the resources necessary to promote your book? Books that languish on warehouse shelves don't pay royalties. And effective promotion increases sales.

4. Is the publisher recognized in your field as a quality publishing house? Quality is a result of strong leadership, skilled editors, effective promotion, and strong products. By reviewing the books they have already published, assess the overall quality of their products. Is this a house with which you wish to be associated? Do they publish authors who are widely recognized in their field? Also assess the quality of their promotion. Do they have an adequate sales force? Do they advertise in the journals you read? Do they use direct mail advertising effectively?

Finding Answers

How would you answer the questions above? You can call upon several resources. For example, make personal contacts. When you attend a professional conference, visit the exhibits and talk with the people staffing the exhibit. Indicate your interest in possibly publishing with that company. If the company uses salespeople, talk with those representatives. Collect publishers' catalogs. Look through each catalog to see what books are listed in your field. Be sure to check copyright dates. Read competing books and analyze their strengths and weaknesses.

UNDERSTANDING THE PUBLISHING PROCESS

If you are thinking about writing a book, you should understand how books are published, because the publishing process has implications for how you write.

Exhibit 9.1 summarizes the major steps in the publication process as they are implemented at Corwin Press, one of the major publishing houses in the field of education. Other houses would follow the same general process, with some variation in the details. The following discussion fleshes out the summary in Exhibit 9.1.

Exhibit 9.1   The Publishing Process

Steps in the Process	Chiefly Responsible
1. Author submits query letter	Author
2. Acquisitions editor encourages author to submit book proposal and sample chapter	Acquisitions editor
3. Author submits book proposal (or book plan) and sample chapters	Author
4. Peer and market reviews commissioned (optional)	Acquisitions editor
5. Book proposal approved, with revisions	Editorial conference
6. Contracts signed	Author, publisher
7. Author submits manuscript	Author
8. Manuscript undergoes critical content review	Developmental editor and peers
9. Manuscript turned over to production department	Production editor
10. Manuscript is copyedited	Copy editor
11. Author makes revisions as requested by copy editor	Author
12. Interior and cover are designed	Book designer
13. Revised manuscript is set in type	Production editor
14. Author reviews typeset pages	Author
15. Book sent to printer for printing	Production editor, printer

First, observe the complexity of the process. Even with minor details omitted, the process still involves 12 separate steps from the time you submit a query letter to the time the book is printed. Note as well that several of the steps involve reviewing and revising. One of the hallmarks of quality publishing is how much time is devoted to reviewing and revising. Finally, note that several members of the publishing staff are involved in the entire process.

KNOWING THE PEOPLE IN THE PROCESS

Eight major functions need to be carried out at the publisher's end; some of these (such as copyediting) might be farmed out to freelancers. Following are the roles typically found in a major house.

The *publisher* is the CEO of the publishing house, ultimately responsible for the success of the company. The *acquisitions editor* is perhaps the most important of all the several editors. He or she is responsible for several key functions: predicting trends in the field, identifying areas needing further development, searching for and developing new authors, reviewing query letters and book proposals, and watching the company's bottom line.

The *developmental editor* is the first of the editors to develop the manuscript after contracts have been signed. These individuals are chiefly concerned with formatting, headings, internal cohesion of the work, and soundness of the content. In smaller houses, the developmental responsibilities are usually outsourced to freelancers.

Peer reviewers may be used at one or two stages. Usually, they are university professors who are experts in the content area. They judge the manuscript in relation to the needs of the market, the currency of the content, and the quality of the references. External reviewers are typically paid a small fee or given one or two books of their choice. (If you would like to be a reviewer, write to the publisher, noting your special area of expertise and enclosing a copy of your resumé.)

Copy editors are like your high school English teacher, correcting errors in sentence structure, word choice, paragraph structure, punctuation, and spelling. When your manuscript has been copyedited, it then goes to the *production editor.* Here are some of the issues that the production editor and copy editor would examine.

- Do titles of chapters as they appear in the book match those listed in the table of contents?

- Do the chapters coordinate well with each other, so that what you said in Chapter 8 supports what you said in Chapter 2?

- Do the references as they appear in the text match exactly with the reference list?

- Are headings formatted correctly, and do they assist the reader in processing the text?

- Have all errors been caught and corrected?

The production editor is a coordinator of sorts, ensuring that the work of the internal staff and the external agents (such as the typesetter and the printer) work together to produce a book in which all can take pride.

Working With Editors

What are the implications of these analyses for would-be authors such as you? Here I draw from two sources. First, Robb Clouse, an excellent acquisitions editor at Corwin Press, has provided some very helpful answers from an editor's point of view. Second, I have drawn upon my own considerable experience in working with editors. Authors should remember that the author and the publishing company are partners, not adversaries. And the editors are the key people in this cooperative relationship. Therefore, it makes sense for the author to establish and nurture a positive relationship. Like all of us, editors need to be stroked.

Be very careful to see that everything you send to the publisher is perfect in form. Editors do not like to deal with error-filled manuscripts. They assume that if an author sends a proposal filled with errors, the author will be careless throughout the process. The acquisitions editor, a key player in increasing the bottom line, knows that carelessness means heavy editing, and editing is very expensive.

Acquisitions editors are also looking for evidence of commitment to the publisher. If an editor suspects that five other publishers are reviewing the same proposal, he or she feels much less positive about it. Authors should make it clear that that publisher is the only one reviewing the proposal.

As an author, I would add just a few reminders of my own.

1. Understand the chain of command. Don't contact the person who is the publisher. Once contracts have been signed, the acquisitions editor will tell you who is your main contact.

2. Meet all deadlines. If it looks as if you will be significantly late in delivering the manuscript as you agreed, let the acquisitions editor know as soon as possible.

3. The editor is right. When differences arise between you and the editor, defer to the editor's judgment. He or she knows the market and brings to the task an objective and informed point of view.

4. If you change the manuscript in a substantive way, do so as soon as possible. Editors are especially unhappy with authors who want to make changes on page proofs. At that stage, major changes will require resetting lines of type and reconfiguring pages.

5. Minimize intrusive contacts with editors. They are very busy people who do not want to be disturbed by overanxious authors.

By reviewing the books the publisher has already published, assess the overall quality of the products. Is this a house with which you wish to be associated? Do they publish authors who are widely recognized in their field?

WRITING THE QUERY LETTER

The query letter is a letter that essentially asks the acquisitions editor, "Are you interested in publishing my book?" Its purpose is simply to explore the level of interest before you write a detailed proposal. A sample query letter is shown in Exhibit 9.2.

Note these points about the letter. It is one page in length. It has three clearly delineated segments: the book, the market, and the author. It is balanced in tone, pointing to the virtues of the work in a somewhat modest tone. It is perfect in form. As Robb Clouse points out, if the query letter is filled with errors, the acquisitions editor will question the writing ability of the author.

Some editors believe that sending a query letter is a waste of time; they wish to see a proposal. Because practice varies here, when in doubt, send the query letter.

Exhibit 9.2   Sample Query Letter

Helen Winstead
Acquisitions Editor
Tampa Publishing Company
316 Central Avenue
Glenside, PA 19038

Dear Ms. Winstead:

All across the nation, forward-looking school systems are implementing new practices designed to foster teacher growth. The major texts in the field of supervision treat these innovative practices in a somewhat superficial manner. Would you be interested in reviewing my proposal for a how-to book designed to help principals and would-be principals design their own system for facilitating teacher growth?

The proposed work has several features that would distinguish it from the competition. I believe that the main selling point is its emphasis on a do-it-yourself approach, because I believe in home-grown models that respond to the special needs of a particular school system. Another feature that will appeal to leaders is the inclusion of working models of these new approaches.

At the present time, there are no books that would compete with the proposed work. In addition to the direct sales market, the book should also sell well as a text for graduate courses in supervision.

As you may know, I am considered an expert in supervision; my book on *Differentiated Supervision,* published by the Association for Supervision and Curriculum Development, has already gone into its second edition.

I have the highest regard for Tampa Publishing Company and hope you are interested in seeing a detailed proposal. I am enclosing a self-addressed stamped envelope to facilitate your reply.

Exhibit 9.3   Elements of the Proposal

1. *The Big Picture:* A description of the book

2. *A Closer Look:* Chapter 1 plus one of your best chapters

3. *Special Features:* What makes this book different

4. *Who's Buying It:* A description of the market

5. *Competition:* What similar books are being marketed

6. *Who Wrote It:* A description of the author's qualifications

DEVELOPING THE PROPOSAL

The proposal is the most important element in the editor's decision to publish or reject. (Some publishers call the proposal a book plan.) In a sense, it is a sales pitch whose main message from the author is, publish me!

Publishers vary in terms of what they require in a proposal. Exhibit 9.3 shows the major elements usually included in the proposal; Exhibit 9.4 is a sample proposal.

A good proposal is characterized by several features. First, it is perfect in form and professional in appearance. Second, it is marketwise; the author demonstrates a current and in-depth knowledge of the market and the competition. Observe that the proposal does not discredit the competition; rather, it lets the data speak. Finally, it describes a book that seems to promise a fresh point of view and the breaking of new ground.

SIGNING CONTRACTS

Let's assume that your proposal is accepted and you receive a contract for the book you proposed. How do you respond? I recommend a middle-of-the-road stance: You should negotiate, remembering that the publisher holds a better hand than you. Should you hire a lawyer? The best answer is to ask an attorney to review the contract, but to do your own negotiating. The main items to negotiate are the following.

Exhibit 9.4   Sample Proposal

Allan A. Glatthorn
Proposal for new supervision book

Working Title

Supervision, No: Growth, Yes

The Big Picture

This book rejects the standard supervision model and, in its place, proposes a new model of teacher growth—a model based on empirical research on how adults change. The book reaches beyond the narrowness of schooling, deriving the new model on the knowledge base from such disciplines as anthropology, adult development, and psychology.

A Closer Look

Chapters 1 and 6 are enclosed.

Special Features

The book distinguishes itself in several ways:

- It enables the principal and the faculty to develop a home-grown model of faculty growth that recognizes the realities of adult growth.

- It presents practical ways to develop and implement new approaches that are effective, such as action research, study groups, and peer coaching.

- It makes meaningful distinctions between teachers at specific levels of development.

Who Is Buying It

There are two major markets. The textbook market is that designed for graduate courses in supervision. Those courses

(continued)

Exhibit 9.4   Sample Proposal (continued)

tend to give superficial attention to such issues as the history of supervision, standard supervisory models, and techniques of supervision. The second market is school principals who are supposed to supervise teachers. They are looking for supervision models that are practical and effective. They want to sharpen their skills.

Competition

The best-selling books in the field are by Alan Greenfield, professor at the University of Georgia, and William Brant, professor of supervision at Virginia Tech. The matrix shown in Exhibit A is an analysis of their works and this proposed work.

Author

Allan Glatthorn is considered one of the top experts in the field of supervision. He has already published three books on supervision. His resumé is attached.

Exhibit A Analysis of Competition

Topic	Greenfield	Brant	Glatthorn
History of supervision	x	x	
Supervision models	x	x	x
Research on standard model		x	x
Rationale for growth model			x
Action research			x
Peer coaching		x	x
Mentoring		x	x
Study groups			x
Creative producing			x
Reflection			x

Royalties

Royalties paid to authors range from 5% to 15%, depending upon publisher policies and the author's ability to produce revenue. Some publishers offer a sliding scale such as this one: 9% on the first 5,000 books sold; 12% on the next 5,000; and 15% on all sales over 10,000. Experts recommend that you negotiate for a fixed rate.

Advances

An advance is an amount of money lent to the author when the contract has been signed. The purpose of the advance is to help the author pay for anticipated expenses during the writing process. Publishers usually will not pay an advance unless the author asks for it; most publishers would prefer to spend their money to promote the book, an advantage to both author and publisher. Consider the advance as a loan. Advances vary from $0 (no advance) to $9,000. Should you request an advance? That depends on many individual factors: your attitudes about loans, your fiscal needs, your work habits, your overall financial picture. If you are still uncertain, don't ask for an advance.

PUBLISHING IN JOURNALS

Publishing in journals is so different from publishing with a commercial publisher that it requires special treatment. The best advice here is "Study the journal." Each journal is aimed at a specific audience; the editor chooses articles on the basis of the article's appeal to the journal's readers.

If you are not sure which journal would be most receptive to your article, here is a process you can use. First, reflect about your article, focusing on the audience you are trying to reach and the type of journal the audience members are likely to read.

Audience is critical. The audiences can be classified into one of several types, as follows, with an example of each.

- Scholars and university professors—*Review of Educational Research*

- School district and school administrators—*School Administrator*

- General educational audience—*Educational Leadership*

- Teachers of a particular subject—*English Journal*

- Teachers and professors specializing in a certain level of schooling—*Elementary School Journal*

At the same time, reflect about the journal's emphasis on research. Scholarly journals publish research reports and reviews of research. Practitioners' journals publish articles on "what works" in schools and classrooms. For example, the editor of *American Educational Research Journal* would not even consider an article on school safety unless it reported on a research study and included multiple references to the research. However, the editor of *Educational Leadership* would give it serious consideration, especially if the editor planned a future issue on school safety.

Here are two examples of the importance of the journal. Ellen Hopkins knows a great deal about school safety because she has completed a dissertation on school safety, with special emphasis on the use of metal detectors. She has decided she wishes to apply for a university position. She decides to submit the article to a research journal because she knows that search committees will be more impressed if her article was published in a research journal.

On the other hand, Jorge Hernandez has developed and tested a comprehensive school safety system. He knows he will find a warm reception if he submits the article to a journal read by school administrators.

With a clear understanding of audience and journals, you should identify five journals of the type you have chosen. You should study those five rather carefully in order to narrow your target to three—one first choice and two stand-by choices. To answer the questions listed below, you can get good information from the specialists in the periodicals section of the university library. You can also search for a recent report by Kenneth Henson, who frequently writes in *Phi Delta Kappan* of his studies of educational journals. Finally, you should read four recent issues of each journal.

1. What are the name and address of the editor? Note that many of the scholarly journals are edited by academics who have a different address from that of the publisher.

2. To what extent do articles cite research? What style is used in citing research?

3. Are submitted articles refereed? Some journals require that articles be evaluated by external reviewers, who are called *referees*. Refereed journals are generally considered more prestigious than nonrefereed journals.

4. Are certain themes identified for future issues? A journal theme is a certain educational issue emphasized by a number of articles on a specific topic.

5. What is the acceptance rate? The acceptance rate is the percentage of articles accepted of those submitted. Journals that have a high acceptance rate are more likely to accept your article. In his 1999 study of educational journals, Henson determined that their acceptance rate ranged from 4% to 80%.

6. What length is preferred? One journal reports that it prefers articles of 1-5 pages; another, 15-20 pages.

7. Does the editor prefer a query letter?

8. Are authors charged a publication fee? Small-circulation journals charge authors a fee, up to $300, to defray publishing costs. Such journals seem less prestigious than the no-fee type.

Obviously, your answers to these questions will influence how you write the article. For specific suggestions about how to write for a practitioner journal, see Chapter 10; for a scholarly journal, Chapter 11.

A CONCLUDING NOTE

Believe in your heart that the educational world is desperately waiting to hear your voice. Don't disappoint them.

REFERENCES

Ross, T., & Ross, M. (1994). *The complete guide to self-publishing* (3rd ed.). Cincinnati, OH: Writer's Digest.

Tabor, M. B. W. (2000, September 24). Big advance? No, he'll publish it himself. *New York Times,* p. BU4.

Van Ryder, B. (1992). Writing groups: A personal source of support. In K. L. Dahl (Ed.), *Teacher as writer* (pp. 34-43). Urbana, IL: National Council of Teachers of English.

PART III

Writing for the Profession

CHAPTER TEN

Writing for Practitioners' Journals

After studying the various venues and publishers, you may decide to submit an article to one of the journals read chiefly by practitioners. What follows is an explanation of how to write such an article and get it published.

STUDY AND SELECT THE JOURNAL

The first step you should take is to study and select a journal. The process is summarized in Box 10.1; it was explained in detail in Chapter 9.

DECIDE ABOUT A QUERY LETTER

By checking the information you have gathered about your preferred journals, determine if the editor prefers a query letter. If so, send a letter similar in organization to the one shown in Box 10.2. Note these points about the sample, which is slightly different from the one about a proposed book shown in Chapter 9.

    1. It suggests that the author reads the journal and considers this journal his or her first choice.

Box 10.1   Selecting the Journal

1. Reflect about potential audience and journal type.

2. Identify and study five likely journals.

   • What are the name and address of the editor?

   • How much research is used, and how is it cited?

   • Are articles refereed?

   • Are themes used?

   • What is the acceptance rate?

   • What length is preferred?

   • Are query letters preferred?

3. Identify your first choice and two standby choices.

---

2. It indicates that there is likely to be a large audience for the article.

3. It describes the article briefly.

4. It explains the author's role.

5. It closes courteously.

BUILD THE KNOWLEDGE BASE

Even if you plan to submit your article to a journal that does not require many references to the research, you should build the knowledge base. Doing so early in the process is a wise move for several reasons. You can determine if the topic is a viable one that still has much current interest. You can get a clear sense of the state of knowledge of this topic. You may decide to challenge conventional think-

Box 10.2   Query Letter: Article for Practitioner Journal

Would you be interested in reviewing an article I have written about school safety? I read in your January issue that you plan a themed issue on this topic for your May issue. Your journal is my first choice.

Despite the fact that school violence has been declining in recent years, there is still a great deal of interest in the topic from school administrators, teachers, and parents. They all know that a case of school violence mishandled can result in a human catastrophe and an organizational disaster.

The article I have written describes a school safety program that is supplemented by a peer mediation approach—a combination that has proved to be effective in our Central Middle School in Dayton, Ohio.

As principal of that school, I have worked with parents, students, and teachers in designing and implementing a multifaceted approach, one that has been rigorously evaluated. The proposed article will be an honest one, describing both our successes and unsolved problems.

Please let me know if you would be interested in seeing the article.

ing. If so, you may have to take more time to build your case. You should know the major figures in the field who are so important that readers will expect you to know their work. Your knowledge of the literature will help you write the query letter and the article itself. And you may decide to develop another perspective or to submit the article to a research journal.

Let's review the steps that I took to increase my knowledge of the topic of school safety so that you may understand some of the decisions you would make. I began by accessing the ERIC database, http://www.askeric.org. I used the two descriptors *school* and *safety,* further limiting the search to the years 1990 to 2000. The computer informed me that it had located more than 2,300 hits by combining these terms. I felt I did not have the time to review all of those. I decided to add the restriction that the desired documents had to include research. Even with all those restrictions, the computer located 382 sources. I decided to review all of them, noting sources that were published in the past 5 years, cited research, and seemed to emphasize practical aspects of the topic. By using those criteria, I located 20 sources that looked very promising. After reading all the abstracts, I selected the 10 that seemed most useful for my article. The last step was to retrieve the full text of those 10. The whole process took about 8 hours, but the search was well worth the time.

WRITE AN EFFECTIVE INTRODUCTION

You should first write an introductory paragraph. Some writers argue that the introduction is a structural component that should not be included in a content outline; however, I have found it to be a useful (albeit illogical) component, reminding me of the special nature of the opening paragraphs. The introduction, then, is a brief opener that tries to accomplish two major objectives: interest the reader, and give the reader a clear understanding of the article's purpose and main ideas. The following discussion is organized in a special way. The opener is given a distinguishing name, the opener is explained briefly, and an example is presented.

- *Shocker:* This opener gets the reader's attention by starting with a dramatic statement.

> Metal detectors are not working. Despite attempts to make the high school look and feel like a jail, the research indicates that these devices are not effective by themselves. Our school has found some options that reduce the violence without making the school jail-like.

- *Organizer:* The organizer gives the reader an overview of the chapter. It is especially effective as an opener for a longer article.

This article is concerned with the growth of the use of metal detectors in secondary schools as a means of reducing violence. It also explains how our faculty decided to supplement the use of metal detectors with a structured program of "school as a learning community." The article concludes with our recommendations to other schools who understand that safety is more than taking all the guns away.

- *Anecdote:* This opener begins with a story, a factual narrative, or a brief anecdote showing the program in action. The narrative makes the article come alive by appealing to the universal enjoyment of stories.

Two 8th graders were fighting in the cafeteria, following an exchange of ethnic insults. Two senior members of the Student Mediation Board quickly separated the combatants and led them to the Mediation Center. That center has helped our school reduce the violence in the school.

- *Question:* The question opener is intended to arouse the reader's curiosity by asking a question whose answer would be illuminating.

Has cooperative learning been oversold as a learning strategy? Our experience has convinced us that it is not a panacea for all students but a useful strategy for many.

- *Thesis:* The thesis is the main idea of the article. Beginning with the thesis adds to clarity but may seem too direct.

Schools must be safe, but there are better ways than metal detectors and security personnel.

As you consider which of these openers you will use, keep in mind that the introduction is often a promise to the reader that you should fulfill. Consider, for example, the paragraph illustrating the "shocker" opener. The author makes two promises. First, he or she will explain why metal detectors alone are not effective. Second, the author promises to explain how the new programs work. The author should fulfill these expectations.

UNDERSTAND THE TYPES OF PRACTITIONER ARTICLES

Understanding the types of articles can help you proceed with the remaining sections of your article. By reviewing several practitioners' journals, I have been able to identify five major types, each of which is discussed below.

Current Trends

An article about current trends is intended to inform the reader about an emerging trend or development. It might carry a title such as "Rethinking Curriculum Alignment." It will usually follow this organizational plan after the opener.

1. *Identification of the Trend:* What is it?

2. *Extent of Trend:* How widespread is it?

3. *Reasons for Growth of Trend:* What factors are causing the trend?

4. *Advantages of Going With the Trend:* How would it benefit your school?

5. *Cautions About Jumping on the Bandwagon:* What potential dangers are there?

Besides using a clear plan, you should keep in mind several other guidelines. First, try to spot a trend before it becomes "old hat." As you probably have observed, educational trends have a short half-life. For example, the block schedule has been so widely adopted that it is difficult to say anything new about it.

Second, particularize by noting in the article your personal experience with the innovations that constitute the trend. What you learned from your direct experience is helpful to other early adopters. Here is an example:

> Although advocates of television as a supervisory tool claim that it is foolproof, they haven't met this fool. On three separate occasions, I have found that after taping a 45-minute class, I have 45 minutes of blank tape.

In writing for a practitioner journal, go easy on the research. Although such journals want a mix of practical experience and sound research, do not be heavy-handed about the research. This excerpt shows what an article sounds like when the research is reported with a heavy hand.

> Glatthorn (1998) has this idea of differentiated supervision. Glickman (2001) calls his model "developmental supervision." Pajak (2000) believes in options but cautions against too much diversity.

Placing the researcher's name at the beginning of each sentence calls too much attention to the researcher. And using the same basic sentence structure exacerbates the problem. The following paragraph is an improvement.

> Several current models stress the importance of options, while differing in details. Differentiated supervision (Glatthorn, 1998) lets teachers choose the type of activity they prefer. Developmental supervision (Glickman, 1984) varies the extent of the structure provided by the supervisor. And what might be termed "organizational supervision" (Duffy, 1987) emphasizes improving the organization.

Finally, practitioners value specificity, because most are reading the article to determine if they will join this trend. Note the difference in these examples:

> *Too vague:* A large number of schools are using models that give teachers a choice of supervisory approach.

More specific: According to a recent survey, 20% of schools participating reported that they were using one of the "options"
models.

Research Summary

Although practitioner journals do not typically feature research,
occasionally they will publish a research summary that challenges the
conventional wisdom or throws light on a current controversy.

Suppose you are writing a research summary focusing on self-
esteem. Here is a simple outline that you might use.

1. Educators believe in many myths with respect to students'
   self-esteem.

2. Myth #1: Self-esteem is a holistic concept; you either have it
   or you don't. The reality: Self-esteem varies in us from area
   to area.

3. Myth #2: Students have low self-esteem. The reality: Most
   students have an inflated sense of self.

4. Myth #3: If you wish to increase students' self-esteem, give
   them more praise. The reality: Teachers praise too much.

5. Myth #4: Higher self-esteem leads to higher achievement.
   The reality: Higher earned achievement leads to higher self-
   esteem.

In developing this article, you would take each of the major
points, note the myth, and refute the myth with the research support,
as in the following:

One of the more pervasive myths held by teachers is an "all-or-
nothing" understanding—to wit, you either have self-esteem or
you don't. Recent research suggests that each person has different levels of self-esteem, depending on the area (see Jorgen,
1998; Wilkins, 1999). Most students understand this concept.
"I'm good in writing stories, but not so good in math" is a typical
student comment.

Keep in mind several cautions in developing the article. First, broaden and deepen your knowledge of the subject, relying chiefly on articles that were published in the past 10 years. Second, remember that educational research is often inconclusive; therefore, use language that is more tentative. These examples show the difference.

Too Conclusive: The research tells us that ability grouping for the gifted is a bad idea.

More Tentative: Because most researchers agree that the research on ability grouping for the gifted is somewhat inconclusive, the reports need to be read with a critical eye.

Even experts in the field reach contrary conclusions about issues such as the following:

- Is increased funding linked to higher student achievement?
- Should nonachieving students be retained in grade?
- Is Reading Recovery effective in teaching beginning reading?

A New Practice

Many articles for practitioners report on a new practice, using a plan like this one:

1. Describe the new practice.
2. Explain its origin.
3. Explain how it works.
4. Identify its strengths and potential problems, drawing upon the research and your experience.

This outline would be useful if you were advocating increased emphasis on physical fitness, rather than sports, for example.

Two points need to be emphasized here. First, be sure that you do not oversell the innovation. Most successful practices have their own problems that should be recognized. For example, too many articles on using the technology ignore such problems as hardware break-downs, excessive costs, necessary training, and obsolescence.

Also, as an aspect of this even-handedness, use language that does not sound like a television commercial. Here are two examples:

> *Claims Too Much:* Our experience with Problem-Based Learn-ing has convinced us that this new learning model constitutes a breakthrough advance in teaching and learning that is highly effective with all students.

> *Makes Tempered Claims:* Our experience with Problem-Based Learning is that, in the hands of well-trained teachers, it can be one of several teaching models that are effective, espe-cially with gifted students.

Attack on Present Practice

Articles attacking some present practice focus on truth-telling, in the writer's view, about some widespread practice that has been over-sold. Here are some sample titles:

Technology Flunks

Cooperative Learning—What They Don't Tell You

Whose Culture Is It Anyway?

In Defense of Social Promotion

As those hypothetical titles suggest, the attack article has a tone of skepticism, asking "Who says?" Ordinarily, such articles use an outline like the following:

1. Evidence of widespread use

2. Claim #1 and its refutation

3. Claim #2 and its refutation

4. Claim #3 and its refutation

5. What we should be doing in its stead

In most attack pieces, the main problem is controlling the tone through careful choice of words. Read this example to decide why and where the tone is inappropriate.

> So now we're back to retention again. President Bush and the governors of many states are recommending a policy of "pass the test or get held back." Now this is a new idea, emerging from the dung heap of educational thinking about 50 years ago. Over these several decades, researchers have conducted numerous studies of the issue, almost always finding that nonachievers who were socially promoted achieved more the next year, had a better self-image, and had a lower dropout rate than peers who were retained. I close with a question: Should we retain educational leaders who don't know or can't apply the research?

TAKE CARE OF THE FINAL DETAILS

Now your tasks are the more pleasant ones of wrapping up and mailing the article. First, as noted previously, get a good proofreader whom you can trust. Correct all errors. Be sure pages are numbered. Address a 9″ × 12″ manila envelope, being sure that you have the correct name and address for the editor. Take it to the post office and send it priority mail.

Once the article has been mailed, forget about it. Don't badger the editor. And wait for the letter that begins, "We are pleased to inform you. . . ."

A CONCLUDING NOTE

For many writers, getting published in a practitioner journal is the first step in the long march to book publication. However, you should write an article addressed to practitioners even if a book does not loom in the distance. Remember—you have a story to tell.

CHAPTER ELEVEN

Writing for Research Journals

Y̲ou may be one of the groups of educators interested in publishing in research journals: researchers working in research institutes, university professors, graduate students, and school practitioners who want to keep up with the latest research. For the most part, they are a very demanding audience, critical of the writing, the reasoning, and the substance of the article. For that reason, publishing in research journals requires special attention. Note as well that doctoral candidates cannot simply submit their dissertations to a journal and hope that they get published. Each journal has its own requirements, and none will publish a dissertation just as it is. For a discussion of the dissertation, read Chapter 17.

TAKE CARE OF PRELIMINARY MATTERS

Three preliminary matters explained in Chapter 10 need attention as well if you are planning to submit an article for a research journal.

• *Study and select the journal.* This step is especially important if you are writing a research article. Even two journals whose titles sound similar may be quite different in what they publish. Consider excerpts from two research journals. According to the *Review of Educational Research,* "[This journal] . . . contains integrative reviews and interpretations of educational research literature on both substantive and methodological issues" (inside cover). On the other hand, the *American Educational Research Journal* is looking for "original reports of empirical and theoretical studies and analyses in education" (inside cover page). If you sent a report of original research to the *Review of Educational Research,* it would probably be rejected out of hand. If you sent a review of the research to the *American Educational Research Journal,* it would not be interested.

In your study of journals, be sure to check the preferred style. Most educational journals prefer that the author use the *Publication Manual of the American Psychological Association* as a style guide.

• *Decide about a query letter.* Because articles submitted to research journals will undergo an intensive evaluation by peers, a query letter may be superfluous.

• *Build the knowledge base.* How much of this you include in the article is determined by several factors. It is much more important to provide a sound knowledge base in the research article than in the practitioner article. How to present the knowledge base is explained below.

FOLLOW GENERAL GUIDELINES

Before examining how to write the specific sections, it would be helpful to lay out some general guidelines about the research article that have been sanctioned by tradition. Note that many of these same issues are discussed in the APA manual (2001), a very useful guide for research articles.

Title

The title should provide a clear clue to the contents, because researchers will examine the title for the possible usefulness of the article. Avoid using such redundant phrases as "a study of" or "an investigation of." The title should appear on the title page. Several years ago, a scholar with a sense of humor published an article on the use of the colon in research articles, having found that a large percentage of research articles used colons, as in this example:

Kitchen Tables as Desks: The Achievement of Home Schoolers

If you are tempted to be clever in writing the title, don't. It is considered bush league.

Authorship

At the outset, you should resolve issues of authorship when the article has multiple authors. The general rule is that authors are listed in relation to their contributions to the article. Thus, if Walker has done most of the work, her name comes first. If Howell has made the second most significant contribution, his name follows Walker's. This matter makes a difference because personnel committees making decisions about tenure and promotion are keenly aware of these distinctions.

Headings

Many writers become confused about headings. This confusion is understandable because the issue is so complex. The APA manual explains how to handle up to 5 levels, each of which varies in its detail. Because a four-level heading is used in most research articles, you should master the formats and punctuation for four-level headings. Here is a quick review of how to handle a four-level set of headings, as previously explained in Chapter 6.

Level 1. If you examine Exhibit 11.1 closely, you will note these features. Level 1 is used for the title. It uses caps and lower case and is not underlined.

Level 2. This heading is used for the major divisions of the article. Observe that it is underlined and centered. A reader should be able to read only the Level 2 headings and be able to say, "The article makes four main points . . ."

Level 3. This is used for the divisions of the Level 2 sections. It is flush left, on a line by itself, and uses caps and lower case.

Exhibit 11.1 Example of Four-Level Heading Style

Level 1	THE MOTIVATING CURRICULUM

One of the most important influences on students' motivation to learn is the curriculum. A qualitative study by Hall (2001) determined . . .

Level 2   School Factors

One reason that it is difficult to raise the level of student motivation is that such levels involve multiple factors.

Level 3   The Hidden Curriculum

Most recently, curriculum theorists have again turned their attention to the study of motivation. In general, they have determined that there are three components of the hidden curriculum that have a great influence.

Level 4   Opportunities for student communication. Students who are in a school that provides multiple opportunities for them to communicate freely with teachers . . .

Level 4. Level 4 is used for divisions of Level 3. Note that it is indented five spaces, uses a capital for only the first word, uses a period at the end of the heading, and does not occupy a separate line.

If you need information for Level 2, Level 3, or Level 5 headings, consult the APA manual.

Length of Article

Another preliminary issue to be resolved by studying the preferred journal is the length of articles published. Be sure that the length of your article falls within the general parameters used by that journal. Some editors prefer that you indicate the number of words in your piece. Check your word processing software; many such programs will give you a word count automatically.

Tone

The tone of an article is similar to tone of voice. With the tone of your voice, you can communicate sarcasm, humility, friendliness, and other attitudes and feelings. You can also communicate tone in writing. First, you should strive for an objective tone in a research article. An objective tone says, in effect, "I am not choosing sides." To achieve an objective tone, suppress expressions of opinion, except in the "Discussion" section, where you are expected to interpret findings. An objective tone can also be achieved through word choice, by avoiding words that are emotionally colored.

Here are some examples of statements that have lost some objectivity:

Harry Jones did a wonderful job checking the statistics for us.

On the day scheduled for interviews, four of the students did not show up at the appointed place, but we did not go for their lame excuses.

We were really happy with the results.

Marty Williams, a great athlete and coach, was most cooperative.

The other tone to work on is suitable modesty and fairness. Modesty here means not calling excessive attention to yourself or not praising your own work. Fairness is crucial in responding to your critics. A few years ago, two well-known researchers got caught in an intemperate debate carried on in the "Letters" section of a nationally read education newspaper. They both lost points by their vitriolic diatribes.

Developing an Outline

In developing an outline, you may decide to follow the traditional order first used in the field of science.

1. Statement of the problem

2. Review of the related literature

3. Methodology

4. Results

5. Discussion

Although widely used for several types of research reports, it does not work for some kinds. Here, for example, is an outline for a report on action research.

1. The problem and its context

2. The methodology for recording actions taken in solving the problem

3. Discussion of the results

In developing this brief outline, the author decided to weave the literature review throughout the article, rather than devoting a separate section to it.

You can construct a "do-it-yourself" outline very simply by referring to Box 11.1. It lists all the components that might be found in a research report and the percentage that each section typically takes. Note, of course, that the percentages are very general estimates, with a great deal of variation. For example, a researcher using a methodology not widely accepted might wish to increase the space devoted to the method used. By reflecting about the story you wish to tell, decide which of the specific components you wish to include, along with the percentage for each. Box 11.2 shows one outline that might be developed with this method. Observe that Box 11.2 does not include a "Definitions" section. Although definitions are often required in a dissertation, they usually are not included in a research article. In using the list of components, keep in mind that it is a comprehensive list of all the items that might be included; you do not have to include everything. For example, many research articles give primary attention to a summary and discussion, minimizing other components.

Box 11.1   Components of the Research Article

Abstract (5%)

  Summary of the article

Introduction (10%)

  Opening paragraphs
  Rationale for and purpose of the study.
  Background and context (may also be placed in the
    Methodology section)
  Theoretical and conceptual framework

Review of Literature (15%)

  Synthesis of related literature

Methodology (20%)

  Type of research
  Context (may also be treated in the introductory section)
  Sample
  Participants
  Methods
  Independent variables
  Dependent variables
  Measures
  Data analysis

Results (25%)

  Findings of the study

Concluding Matters (25%)

  Summary of the results
  Discussion
  Conclusions
  Recommendations
  Implications
  Limitations

**Box 11.2   Outline Developed From Selected
Components**

---

1. Abstract

2. Rationale and significance

3. Review of literature

4. Methodology

5. Results

6. Summary and discussion

WRITE THE ABSTRACT

Most research journals require you to begin with an abstract. An abstract is a 100- to 200-word summary of the entire article. Using an abstract enables readers to determine quickly if that article is sufficiently important to save. Exhibit 11.2 shows an abstract of an article appearing in the *American Educational Research Journal* (Fall, 1999). Note that it includes one or two sentences about four essential elements: purpose of the study, methods, results, and discussion. Although the abstract appears first in the outline, you may wish to write it last so that you have all the data needed.

WRITE THE INTRODUCTION

The introduction is that matter that appears before you identify the problem of the study. The introductory section may be as brief as one paragraph or as long as several pages. The length depends on the extent to which readers are informed about the topic. In his article on Ebonics, Ogbu (1999) devotes several pages to the theoretical background, because his readers are probably not well informed about the subject. Unlike the practitioner article, the research article need not be chiefly concerned with enticing readers to read.

Exhibit 11.2 Example of Abstract

The purpose of this study was to examine effects of classroom-based performance-assessment (PA)-driven instruction. Sixteen teachers were randomly assigned to PA and no-PA conditions. PA teachers attended a workshop, administered 3 PAs over several months, and met with colleagues to score PAs and share ideas for providing student feedback and instruction. PA teachers' knowledge about PA increased; their curriculum shifted toward problem solving; and they reported relying on varied strategies to promote problem solving. Compared to no-PA students, above-grade PA students showed stronger problem solving on all measures; at-grade PA students, on 2 of 3 measures; below-grade students, on only 1 dimension of 1 measure. Professional development needs to promote mathematical problem solving among all students are discussed.

SOURCE: Fuchs, L. S., Fuchs, D., Karns, K., Hamlett, C. L., & Katzaroff, M. (1999). Mathematics performance assessment in the classroom: Effects on teacher planning and student problem solving. *American Educational Research Journal, 36*(3), 609-646.

The introduction includes one or more of the following components.

Context for the Study

The context of the study helps the reader understand the environment in which the study was undertaken. Typically, it includes one or more of the following elements:

1. When and where did the study take place?

2. What was happening in education at the time of the study?

3. Who was involved in the study?

Here is an example of a description of the context.

At the time of this study, 48 states had produced curriculum or content standards to assist school systems in building challenging curricula that embody a common core of significant learnings. At the same time, every professional association had developed its own set of standards. This plethora of standards resulted in the hasty production of standards-based curricula. In general, the quality of these curricula was judged to be only "satisfactory" by a panel of evaluators.

Purpose of the Study

The purpose of the study explains why the study was undertaken. Here are some ways the purpose can be stated:

The study reported here was undertaken to determine if remedial interventions were effective with students being retained in grade.

The purpose of this study was to determine if there were significant differences in the mathematics achievement of varsity athletes as compared with that of nonathletes.

The object of this study was to ascertain if teachers who were provided five after-school workshops in unit planning produced better quality units than did teachers not attending the workshop.

A Theoretical or Conceptual Framework for the Study

Much research is undergirded with a theoretical analysis or a conceptual framework. A theoretical analysis delineates the theory that provided a basis for the study. For example, Ogbu's (1999) study of "Black English," or "Ebonics," devoted six pages to the theories of social linguistics before discussing methodology and results. A theoretical analysis is usually explained with text accompanied by a visual representation. A sound theory has some clear advantages for you. It provides a useful background, suggests areas you might investigate, and helps you organize your literature review.

A conceptual framework is often derived from the theoretical analysis. You identify the main concepts and then show visually how they are related. The conceptual framework is a visual summary of concepts and their relationships. Consider, for example, the concep-

Figure 11.1. Conceptual Framework: Academic Motivation

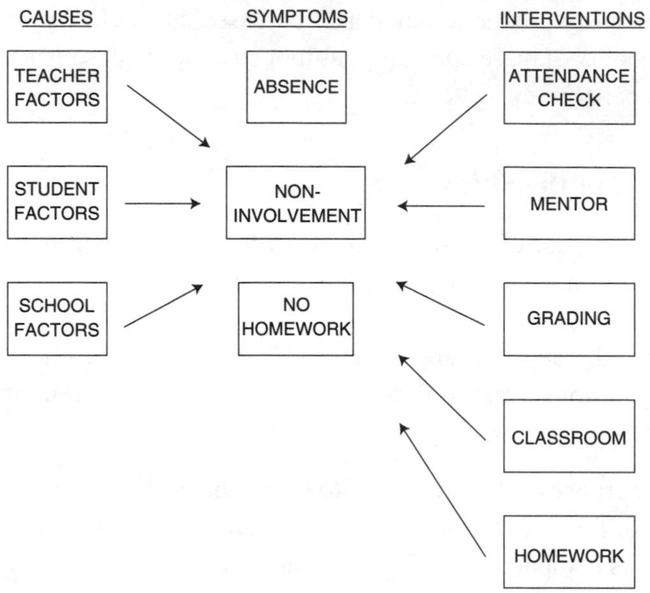

tual framework for a discussion of motivation shown in Figure 11.1. It should enable you to understand what major factors influence student motivation and how they are related. Once you understand the theory of a particular phenomenon, you select the major concepts and then decide how you will represent their relationships.

Definitions

You may decide to include in your research article the definitions of key terms. For the most part, however, definitions should be used in a dissertation but not in the research article. If you do include definitions, follow these simple guidelines:

- Define only those terms that readers of the journal are not likely to know and those terms that you use in a special sense.

- Use your own definition of a given term, or borrow one (with suitable acknowledgment).

- If you define the term with a dictionary definition, avoid saying, "According to Webster. . . ." Instead, use the same form you use with the rest of your references. Here is an example of a clear definition:

Accountability is an organizational system that assigns specific responsibilities to an individual or group, expecting that person or group to report on the discharge of responsibilities. Typically, it includes several additional components: an assessment process, a delineation of the results obtained, a system of rewards and sanctions, and full public disclosure.

REVIEW OF THE LITERATURE

You will include in your research article a review of the literature, not just because it will impress an editor, but because it will also provide a basis for your own research. A basic tenet of the scientific tradition is that scientific knowledge is cumulative, with one study building upon what has gone before.

Selecting the Studies to Be Reviewed

One critical step is to select the articles to be reviewed. You want to call attention to the best studies in the field, not every study you were able to lay your hands on. Here are some criteria to use in judging research reports:

1. *Current.* The research was published no more than 10 years ago, unless the research has historical significance.

2. *Sound in design.* The research was conducted according to sound design and valid methods.

3. *Objective.* There is no evident bias in the article.

4. *Substantive.* The findings are important to the field.

Planning the Review

Once you have selected the sources to include, your next task is to make some key decisions about organizing them.

Separate or Integrate. The first decision you have to make is whether to write a separate section titled "Review of the Literature," or whether to integrate the literature review with the rest of the text. To answer this question, check the practice of the research journal to which you plan to submit. Also consider the previous research itself. If that literature is voluminous, the separate section will probably work better. On the other hand, if only a few studies have been done, an integrated review might have greater appeal.

Organize the Separate Review. If you decide to write an integrated review, the decision about its organization is relatively simple: Specific studies are cited as your own study calls for them. However, if you write a separate review, then you have to decide how to organize that section. Here you have a few choices. First, you may organize the section chronologically according to the date of publication. This plan is especially useful if there have been significant changes in the research over a period of time.

Second, you can use a "pro-con" pattern if the research seems divided in its conclusions. Thus, if you were reviewing the literature on social promotion, you might have two subsections: research supporting social promotion, and research opposing social promotion. Finally, you can use a topical pattern in which you organize the section in relation to its big ideas. Here you should find your conceptual framework to be of use. Discuss the literature by reviewing the material on each topic, noting each set of relationships. The key idea here is to organize clearly in a manner that simplifies the readers' task.

Writing the Literature Review

As you write the review of the literature, keep in mind the following general guidelines. First, synthesize—don't just list. Your readers want to see your mind at work, evaluating and synthesizing major sources. Novice writers simply list studies, often in a random pattern. A skilled writer takes five studies and makes some sense out of them.

Contrast these two excerpts.

Example of a Poor Review

Corno (1992) sees motivation as having several components, including a goal orientation. Ames (1990) notes how important it is for teachers to understand student motivation to learn. If you don't understand it, you can't change it. One of the factors influencing student motivation is the parents. Lumsden (1999) argues that parents have a great influence, as do Wlodskowski and Jaynes (1990). There are a lot more to consider.

Example of a Good Review

Researchers have identified several major factors influencing motivation to learn; it seems helpful to note that only one of those factors is external to the student, thus challenging those educators who believe that senior proms and football games are motivating to those not participating in them. The one external factor influencing student motivation to learn is the parents. Parent support manifests itself in many ways. . . .

Note that the poor review exhibits several flaws. It simply lists reports without a synthesis. The writer has not made sense of the literature. Also, too many sentences begin with the researchers' name and date of publication. In addition, the review uses language that is too colloquial. Here are some examples of other ways to gain variety and avoid putting the researcher's name first:

According to Corno (1990) . . .

As reported by Corno (1990) . . .

Motivation involves multiple components (Corno, 1990).

Motivation, as Corno (1990) notes, is . . .

Motivation is multifaceted. (See Corno, 1990).

Remember that you may decide the paper would be more effective if the literature review was integrated throughout the article. Here is an example:

> One of the findings with clear implications for practice is that most students seem to have an inflated sense of their academic abilities. This finding has also been reported by Swanson (2000) and by Shermorman (2002).

EXPLAIN THE METHODOLOGY

One of the traditions of scientific inquiry is to present in the research report a detailed explanation of the methods used. Doing so accomplishes two objectives: It enables the reader to replicate that research, and it helps readers to evaluate the soundness of the research.

In explaining the methodology, select only those components that would enable the readers to replicate your study. Not all need to be included; each research approach has its own set of required methodological components. You also must decide how to organize this section. Typically, you begin by identifying the general research approach. You then organize the rest of the components in chronological order, discussing them in the order in which they usually are undertaken.

Here is an example of a portion of a description of the methodology:

> The research design combined qualitative and quantitative methods. Access to the research site was relatively simple to obtain because the principal and the superintendent had previously worked with and seemed to trust the research team. Five English teachers volunteered to participate in the study. The qualitative aspect of the study consisted of a focus group interview of these teachers. The interviews were transcribed. The transcriptions were then analyzed to identify recurring themes. . . .

REPORT THE RESULTS

Several issues are at play in reporting the results. First, consider the organization of this section. If you expressed the problem as a series of questions to be answered, organize the results by answering the questions. If your first problem question was "How do teachers perceive the motivation levels of their students?" then your readers expect to see that question answered first.

When the literature review suggests that opinions are sharply divided, you could use a "for" and "against" order. Suppose, for example, that your study examined the issue of ability grouping for the gifted. You might have two longer sections: studies supporting ability grouping for the gifted, and studies questioning ability grouping for the gifted. You could also organize the results section by participants: results of the teacher survey, and results of the student survey. Also qualitative studies may use a chronological framework: findings at the midpoint of the study, and findings at the end of the study.

Reporting Statistical Results

Statistical results are best reported in tables and figures. A table is a structured presentation of data, usually reported in columns and rows. A figure is a line drawing, graph, or illustration. (I use the term "box" in this book to identify a set of closely related findings or a summary of complex information.) There are some general guidelines in handling tables and figures. Because tables and figures are typeset separately, they should be placed at the end of the manuscript, with a note in the text indicating where they should be presented in the printed book. The following example shows how to handle this issue:

As Figure 12.2 indicates, four elements seemed to affect administrators' judgments.

Remember that the tables and figures are used to clarify and simplify data. In writing the textual commentary, do not simply repeat information presented in the table or figure.

Exhibit 11.3 Example of Summary Section

This article reports the results of an interview study of 20 middle school teachers. The study focused on the perceptions of those teachers with respect to the positive and negative effects of high-stakes tests.

Twenty teachers assigned to the middle schools of Bryant school system were chosen at random and organized into four focus groups of five each. Each group was interviewed for 2 hours, using an interview protocol developed by the researcher. Interviews were audiotaped, with permission of the teachers. Tapes were transcribed for more exact analysis. The analysis focused on finding recurring patterns.

In general, the teachers interviewed manifested an attitude of reluctant acceptance of the tests as an unpleasant element in their professional lives. Their specific concerns focused on the tests as an intrusive aspect. In their perceptions, preparing for the tests caused them to narrow the curriculum to the tested content areas. They also reported that preparing for and administering the tests caused them to lose instructional time. Finally, most of the teachers expressed concerns about the negative effects of the tests on students.

SUMMARIZE AND DISCUSS THE RESULTS

This last section of the research article is, in many ways, the most important part of the entire report. It typically includes two major components: the summary, and the discussion. Be sure that it tells your story.

Summary

Write the summary first by summarizing the major parts of the methodology. Do not summarize the literature. Then, summarize the major findings, rather than all the details. Do not include tables or figures. Exhibit 11.3 presents an example of a summary.

Discussion

The discussion presents you with the opportunity to interpret the findings—to make sense of the study. In doing so, you should find the following process useful when writing the discussion.

Begin by reviewing your results, making notes about the results that seem to need some interpretation. Keep in mind these questions that readers might have:

- What contribution has your study made to the existing knowledge base? How do your results build upon and extend the professional knowledge?

- How do you explain any seemingly contradictory findings?

- To what extent do your findings support or disagree with previous work?

- What are the implications of your findings for educational practice?

Begin the discussion section by interpreting the general conclusion of the study. Give the reader the big picture before the details. The following excerpt is an example of how to accomplish that goal.

The general finding, as noted above, is that teachers reluctantly accept high-stakes tests as a necessary evil. As one of the teachers said, "Why fight the state? They have all the power." Perhaps the most likely explanation of this attitude is that teachers in this state have had a long history of state control over both curriculum and assessment.

After discussing the general conclusion, turn to any specific findings that seem to require interpretation, as the following excerpt does.

The finding that the teachers interviewed cared most of all about the loss of instructional time replicates that of other studies (see Giles, 2001; Johnson, 2000; Walker, 1995). Middle school teach-

Exhibit 11.4 Portion of "Discussion" Section

DISCUSSION

Described here is a case of *assessment paralysis* created by the
tension between a call for change in curriculum and pedagogy
on the one hand, and mandated tests that still reflect simplistic
views of learning and curriculum on the other. Teachers' percep-
tion of an externally defined assessment and curriculum, com-
bined with their limited understanding of mathematics and the
process of learning it, results in limited summative assessment
practices that emulate those imposed by state-mandated assessment. . . .

Through discussions with other educators about curriculum
reform, teachers are receiving the message that they need to focus on meaningful, relevant, conceptual understandings in their
teaching. At the same time, they still feel accountable for producing the same indicators of student success as measured by
scores on mandated tests. . . .

A key element in this study concerns the difficulty that all
three teachers had in reconceptualizing mathematics. The
teachers were aware of their limited understanding of mathematics and acknowledged their need for models and ways to re-
think their teaching and assessment.

The main implication here concerns the education of teachers, their continued learning, and their disposition toward learning. A certain complacency exists about not knowing, particu-
larly in mathematics, an area in which for some it has become
intellectually and socially acceptable to declare one's ignorance. In venturing away from the traditional textbooks, as the
teachers in this study were preparing to do, considerable assistance (e.g., professional development, mentoring) will be
needed to avoid spending substantial amounts of time in ac-

(continued)

Exhibit 11.4 Portion of "Discussion" Section (continued)

---

tivities devoid of disciplinary content. The criteria that these teachers envisioned to assess performance on new activities seemed alarmingly generic, not taking into account knowledge of the discipline.

SOURCE: Delandshere, G., & Jones, J. H. (1999). Elementary teachers' beliefs about assessment in mathematics: A case of assessment paralysis. *Journal of Supervision and Curriculum, 14,* 216-240.

---

ers in this school system are reported to be conscientious professionals who worry about any loss of teaching time.

One final reminder about writing the discussion section is to use the language of tentativeness. Because you are reporting your interpretations, you should avoid dogmatic assertions. Instead, use such locutions as the following:

It may well be that . . .

Possibly . . .

One clear inference is that . . .

One could speculate that . . .

It might be inferred that . . .

Exhibit 11.4 is part of an excellent discussion in a research article by Delandshere and Jones (1999). Note both the tentative language and their helpful interpretations.

A CONCLUDING NOTE

Aside from using this chapter, perhaps the best way to learn how to write research articles is to read 10 or more from different journals, noting especially how the best ones are organized. Also, look closely at how the summary and discussion are handled.

REFERENCES

American Psychological Association. (2001). *Publication manual of the American Psychological Association* (5th ed.). Washington, DC: Author.

Delandshere, G., & Jones, J. H. (1999). Elementary teachers' beliefs about assessment in mathematics: A case of assessment paralysis. *Journal of Supervision and Curriculum, 14,* 216-240.

Ogbu, J. U. (1999, Summer). Beyond language: Ebonics, proper English, and identity in a black American speech community. *American Educational Research Journal, 36* (2), 147-184.

CHAPTER TWELVE

Writing the Opinion Piece

W hat is your opinion—about charter schools, school improvement, safe schools? As an educational leader, you have a responsibility to try to influence policymakers and other educators by writing opinion pieces on timely issues of importance. There are several outlets for cogently reasoned and well-written articles expressing your opinion: *Education Week,* your local newspaper, letters to the editor of educational journals, letters sent directly to policymakers, and the Internet.

HANDLING PRELIMINARY MATTERS

You should first take care of several preliminary matters. Begin by checking your impulse to write. The main problem with writing is that it is so permanent. I have gotten into trouble by writing and sending letters that I should have thrown into the wastebasket. Here are some of the occasions when your impulse to express your opinion in writing should be checked twice.

- You would report information that is supposedly confidential.

- You don't understand the issue or are not sufficiently informed about it.

- You want to entertain your readers and impress them with your wit. Humor does not travel well and is open to misunderstanding.

- You have an unpopular opinion and work for a boss who believes that everyone should follow the party line. If you have tenure and don't mind taking the heat, you can ignore this admonition of caution.

You also check the topic as part of the preliminary reflection. Ask yourself the following questions.

- *Is it a controversial issue?* There is general agreement that cooperative learning is effective. Thus, it would not be a suitable topic unless you wanted to question its overuse.

- *Is it timely?* Educational fads do not last very long. Write about a hot topic, not a cold one. Thus, Outcomes Based Education seems to have had its day, even though it had several sound components. At this time, your opinion about it would not interest many educators.

- *Is it of interest to me?* You can write better when you have strong feelings about it. Lukewarm advocacy does not persuade.

If you are convinced that you want to write about this topic, then analyze the outlet you have chosen, considering these factors.

1. Does it publish opinion pieces?

2. If so, what is the average length of opinion pieces?

3. How formal is the style of opinion pieces?

4. Are opinion pieces documented and referenced? If so, which style manual is used?

It is especially crucial to analyze the audience. Can you guess where they stand on the issue? Research indicates that readers who are uncertain about which side to take are more influenced if a rebuttal is included. For example, if you are advocating the extension of the charter school movement and you believe your readers are uncertain about the issue, you should rebut the arguments of those opposed to charter schools. Also reflect about which arguments are likely to appeal to your audience. For example, are they more likely to be swayed by financial reasons or by arguments based on student achievement?

Take time as well to build the knowledge base. Opinions supported by research are more likely to influence most readers. Consider these two examples:

No Research Cited

I do not believe that retaining students in grade is a helpful strategy for improving the achievement of slow learners. Students who have learning problems need special assistance, not the stigma of retention. I have known retained students who did less well after retention than they did the first time around. At the same time, they seemed to lose a measure of self-confidence.

Research Cited

I do not believe that retaining students in grade is a helpful strategy for improving the achievement of slow learners. My opinion on this issue has been derived from 50 years of research. The preponderance of these studies conclude that students who were socially promoted achieved more than those who were retained. (See Irving, 2001, for a very useful review.)

Recommending the use of research to support your arguments does not mean that you should ignore your experiential learning. An opinion piece that mixes research and experience is probably most effective.

The final preparation you should make is to decide how you should organize your opinion piece. Here are some guidelines:

1. Begin with an opening that will interest your readers.

2. Include a rebuttal if you think many of your readers are undecided.

3. In most cases, you should not identify more than three arguments supporting your position. Most readers cannot keep more than three in mind.

4. If you have three arguments for your position and one is weaker than the other two, put the weaker reason in the middle and the strongest at the end.

5. Write an effective closing.

The following is a rough outline that follows these guidelines.

Introduction

Rebuttal

Second Strongest Reason

Weakest Reason

Strongest Reason

Conclusion

Here is another that is slightly different.

Introduction

Second Strongest Reason

Weakest Reason

Strongest Reason

Rebuttal

Conclusion

WRITING THE INTRODUCTION

Remember that the introduction has two major purposes: to interest the readers, and to state the main idea. If you are writing about a complex issue that has changed over the years in its essentials, you may wish to include the background of the issue. In most opinion pieces, the main idea is stated in one of three different places.

Here are three examples you might consider. Does one appeal more than the others?

Main Idea First

Too many educators are jumping too quickly on the "brain-based learning" bandwagon. In my view, the bandwagon is lost, careening from place to place with no clear sense of direction.

This direct beginning should be used when the opinion piece is relatively short and the issue simple. To many readers, it may sound too direct.

Main Idea at End of First Paragraph

The last time I counted, there were 18 books in print dealing with the topic of "brain-compatible learning" as it applied to school learning. And each month, I receive a brochure explaining that I must attend a conference on the brain, led by all the stars of the consulting circuit. In my view, all this mindless activity is misdirected.

Putting the main idea at the end of the first paragraph avoids being too direct while still identifying the main idea in the opening paragraph.

Background First, Main Idea in Second Paragraph

For many decades, we educators joined the crowd who saw the brain as a black box that defied the best efforts of scientists to open. Then there came a time when we eagerly embraced the preliminary finding that the brain had two distinct sides, each with special functions. Do you remember all that talk about using your right brain? Now we seem to be in an era when some educators believe that the black box has been opened and all its mysteries laid bare.

Unfortunately, the box is still closed, and all the talk about "brain-based learning" is misdirected.

This beginning is useful if you are writing a longer piece and have patient readers. Do not let the background section run too long, however.

STATING YOUR ARGUMENTS

You can use several patterns in stating your arguments. Here is one that seems to work well.

1. Reflect about your audience and identify just a few arguments that would work best with them. You can give one extended reason, although offering only one makes you seem vulnerable to attack. You probably should use two, three, or four reasons. Five would probably be too many.

2. Write a topic sentence that you place first or second in your paragraph. Here is an example: Incremental change, as opposed to systemic change, requires fewer resources.

3. Develop that topic sentence by using several strategies. You can use logical reasons, cite statistics, quote experts, or tell anecdotes. The choice of method is of little consequence; all that counts is the overall effectiveness of your arguments. The topic sentence above might be developed as follows:

> Because such resources as personnel, time, and funds seem always to be in short supply in schools, any change process that minimizes the use of these elements is likely to have more appeal to teachers. Consider staff development time as only one instance of resource availability. A faculty used to working together might need only four staff development sessions to acquire the skills involved in curriculum alignment. On the other hand, several articles report how a given school faculty has become bogged down in what seem to be an endless round of meetings and meetings about meetings.

WRITING THE REBUTTAL

An effective rebuttal has several features. First, it states the position of the opposing side without distortion. If quotations are used, they are reported with fidelity and accuracy. The rebuttal also uses a professional tone marked by courtesy and rationality. You should not use ridicule to make your points. Finally, it is constructively critical; readers bristle when they encounter too much negativity. Here is an example of a portion of an effective rebuttal:

> One argument of learning styles advocates is that accommodating learning styles results in higher achievement. There are several troublesome concerns with the research cited here. First, the concept of "learning styles" is used with so many different meanings that it is difficult to know what is intended. Second, many of the instruments used to identify preferred learning styles have been poorly designed, with no published data available on validity and reliability. Finally, most of the research supporting accommodation has been carried out by doctoral students working under the direction of faculty members who have a vested interest in such programs. This is not to charge them with dishonesty but to warn them about the dangers of unconscious bias.

WRITING THE CONCLUSION

You have several options for your concluding paragraph. First, you can simply end with your strongest point, with no conclusion as such. This should work with shorter pieces. Second, you can write a brief exposition of the implications of your arguments or a delineation of the next steps that should be taken, as in the following example.

> These reservations about learning styles programs do not mean that teachers should totally reject these programs. They seem to have enough support to recommend that school administrators and teachers should continue to examine their merits, read current research, and help students write more effectively.

You can also close by writing a summary, especially for a longer article, as this paragraph does:

> What can be said in summary? I have expressed grave concern about the leap that teachers make, jumping from rats in a maze to children in classes. I have criticized the inflated language used by its advocates to describe useful teaching strategies—strategies as old as John Dewey's liberal approach. And I have encouraged all educators (including this one) to keep an open mind about brain-based learning and all its derivatives.

Many other strategies can be used, of course. The important matter is to leave the reader with a sense of closure.

REVISING AS NECESSARY

In revising an opinion piece, keep in mind several criteria. Ask the following questions as you read an early draft.

Does this opinion piece . . .

1. Use effective arguments in a way likely to persuade the audience?

2. Conform to the requirements of the journal?

3. Show adaptation to the audience in content, language, and sentence structure?

4. Use an organization that is clear and reader-centered?

5. Include rebuttal where appropriate?

6. Present arguments that are well supported?

7. Begin and end effectively?

8. Exhibit a tone that is reasonable and professional?

This last matter of tone requires special sensitivity on the part of writers of opinion pieces. A reasonable tone is one based on the real-

ization that there are no final answers in education. A professional
tone is one that respects the audience. Consider these examples:

Appropriate Tone

There is no intent here to ridicule teachers who are doing their
best to interest students in the work at hand by using effective
strategies labeled "brain based." Regardless of the label, it makes
good sense to provide variety in the classroom.

Inappropriate Tone

I feel sorry for the poor teachers who have succumbed to the
blandishments of the "experts" on the brain. I also pity these so-
called experts who do not use in their workshops techniques recommended in their books. I call them brain-based charlatans.

A CONCLUDING NOTE

I obviously have a bias here. I believe that professionals have a responsibility to publish their views on the major issues that face educators today. Such expressions, presented effectively, can gradually
bring about positive changes in the public climate.

CHAPTER THIRTEEN

Writing the Big Book

S et your sights high. Write the big book that will make its mark in your profession. Don't be intimidated by the size and complexity of the task. Like any long journey, it is made one step at a time.

What are the separate steps in producing an excellent book? To begin with, you would be wise to review Chapter 9 because it contains much that would be helpful to you in publishing your book. This chapter answers three general questions: How do you get ready? How do you write the book? How do you promote your book once it has been published?

GETTING READY TO WRITE

Several preparatory steps are essential if you are going to write a successful educational book.

Finding Time to Write

Writing takes time. Good writing takes more time. And writing good books takes even more. One answer to the "I don't have the time" excuse is, "You have the time if you schedule it well." Here is one way to schedule time.

1. *Protect large blocks of time.* I need a good 4-hour block twice a week if I am to make the progress I desire. If you work or study full-

Box 13.1   Writing Schedule

Dates	Major Events	Book Task	Date Completed
3/1-3/7	Family visit	Query letter	3/14
3/8-3/14	Income taxes	Begin knowledge building	3/28

time and are part of a loving family, perhaps you will have to make do with one 4-hour block. Brief the family about your writing schedule and solicit their cooperation. My family knows that when I retreat to the study, I do not wish to be disturbed. Of course, whether or not they always accede to those wishes is another matter.

2. *Make a realistic schedule.* With some sense of how much time you can defend, you should next make a schedule. Lay out a writing schedule similar to the one in Box 13.1. Box 13.2 is an alternative form you might prefer. The schedule assumes that you can find 8 hours each week for your writing and that you have signed a contract. One point to keep in mind if you are writing a textbook is that textbook publishers want a finished product that they can market during the adoption period, which runs from January to March for texts to be used in the fall term. Most publishers work on a schedule that requires 9 months of turnaround time. That means you should deliver a finished manuscript in early spring.

Here are some general guidelines about the time required for each major step.

Step	Time Required
1. Build knowledge base	16 hours for each chapter
2. Write first draft of chapter	24 hours for each chapter
3. Revise chapter	12 hours
4. Revise entire manuscript	16 hours

Box 13.2 Alternative Scheduling Form			
February	*March*	*April*	*May*
Chapter 1 initial draft	Chapter 1 revision	Chapter 2 draft	Chapter 2 revision

Obviously, there will be much individual variation, because the time allocations depend on several factors difficult to predict: knowledge of subject, ability to concentrate and sustain a good tempo, complexity of the book, and writing ability. Therefore, it makes good sense for you to develop your own realistic schedule that builds in some flexibility for the unpredictable.

Deciding on the Type of Book

For the purpose of planning the work, you need to choose which of three types you will write.

Assembling a Book. The assembled book is one you write by assembling or pulling together your previous writing. For doctoral students, that means cannibalizing your dissertation and turning it into a book proposal. For instructors, it is revising your class notes and handouts. For a previously published author, it can be a way of assembling the best of the past.

Assembling a book can be useful to those who are concerned chiefly with loading a resumé with the titles of several books. However, there are several problems. One is the ethical issue: It is dishonest to pass off as a new work what has already been published. Second, assembling a book might be illegal if the publisher holds the copyright for your previously published work. Finally, there is the quality issue. Assembled books are likely to be dated, because they are drawing from your past works. I recommend assembling a book only in these instances: You are a famous educator whose old works are worth reading, you have published some wonderful pieces that never got the attention they deserved, or you face a tenure/promotion review and you don't have time to do a fresh book.

Editing a Book. One very useful means of breaking into print is to edit a book that includes several chapters written by others. First, you need to choose a subject for the book. Let's say that you decide to edit a book on violence in the schools, with an international perspective. You make a rough outline, analyzing the topic to identify the big questions. Then, you assemble the author team. You want to find writers who can meet deadlines, write effectively, and see beyond the obvious. You search the Internet and check the reference lists of major works recently published. That will provide you with several good leads. To get more credit and to give you more control over the work, consider saving the first and last chapters for yourself.

Then you wait. Chapters dribble in, one each month for the most part. You make several discomfiting discoveries. Of the 12 authors you invited, 2 turn you down. Two more submit chapters that need heavy editing. Four chapters are publishable. The other four authors do not submit chapters; they submit excuses.

My experience in serving as editor for such works has led me to develop this principle: The quality of a book is inversely proportional to the number of individuals who have worked on it. The other drawback is that tenure/promotion committees are generally not much impressed by a book that the individual under review has only edited.

Writing Your Own Book. This is the preferred choice. You conceptualize the book. You write the book. You revise the book. It's your book, and you take responsibility for it.

Determining the Topic

You probably have some general idea about the focus of your planned book. If you still are uncertain, you might find these questions useful in finding a focus.

1. *What do you care about?* Writing is enervating, drawing much upon your internal resources. Therefore, you will write better if you burn with an inner zeal about the topic. You can, of course, have

so much enthusiasm that you lose your objectivity, but the excessive zeal can be curbed. It is much more difficult to generate enthusiasm about a topic that does not really matter to you.

2. *What do you know?* The more you know, the better you write. Reflect about your experiential knowledge. What have you learned? To what extent are you up-to-date on the empirical research?

3. *Is the topic timely?* Timeliness involves the extent to which the topic will still be of interest to the profession. As you are probably aware, short-lived fads are common in education. This faddism means that your planned book should hit the market when the fad is in its beginning stages.

Organizing Your Storage and Retrieval System

By this time, you will probably be ready to systematize your information processing and your writing. How you store and retrieve information is an idiosyncratic process. However, a few general suggestions may be of use to you. First, you will need to organize your information files. These are the files in which you store all the articles you will use in writing the book. Photocopy all articles that look useful. Be sure to get full bibliographic information: author; title of article; name of journal; volume number; date; page numbers for the article. Write this information on the first page of the photocopy. For books, write a brief summary that you can slip into the book, and shelve the book close to your writing station. I do not recommend that you use note cards; I find them difficult for both storing and retrieving information. Use any system that works for you. I have been searching for software that will facilitate the process, but so far, I have not found anything that meets my needs, nor anything written in English rather than computerese.

You also should organize a writing file. My system is to dedicate one 3-inch disc for each book I am writing or have written. All the chapters and related materials for one book are stored on one disc. I make a separate file for each chapter and copy all the chapters to my hard drive. Mark one additional file as "front matter," and identify one other as "publisher/editor." The file for front matter includes prefatory sections, as explained later. The publisher/editor file includes the contract, publisher guidelines, and editorial correspondence.

Determining the Audience

Another key decision is to identify and analyze the audience. Your book will likely get a warmer reception if you tailor your book to the needs and interests of the expected audience. The decision about audience will affect both content and writing style.

Here are some questions you should ask about the likely audience:

1. What is the professional role that the audience members occupy?

2. Are they interested primarily in research, practice, or a mix of the two?

3. Do they prefer shorter pieces, or will they sit still for in-depth analyses?

4. How much knowledge do they have about the topic?

Summarize what you have learned, and file the summary under "Audience."

Building the Knowledge Base

Review the research on the topic. Make it a comprehensive review that includes dissertations, research reports, and research syntheses. Should you include the names and addresses of schools that have been implementing successfully the innovation you are recommending? This information is especially important if you are writing for an audience of school administrators and teachers. If you decide to refer to a particular school or individual, be sure to get permission.

Developing the Table of Contents

With all of the information you have gathered, you should be able to finalize the table of contents. Take your time with this step. It is crucial for two reasons: Editors reviewing your proposal will look very critically at the table of contents, and most potential readers will skim the table of contents to determine if they wish to buy the book.

Consider a three-stage process in finalizing the table of contents. In Stage 1, conceptualize the main divisions of the book. Review competing works. Reflect about your audience's needs. Determine which big ideas you will treat. Then, turn to Stage 2. Review the table of contents you developed for the proposal. Take each section and develop the specific chapters under each section heading. Finally, note the topics you will treat in each chapter. You may find it easier to do the Stage 3 analysis when you have finished writing the chapters. You simply list the main headings you have used in each chapter.

Analyzing the Competition

A key part of any proposal is the analysis of competing books. The acquisitions editor can usually help you by identifying the market leaders in your area. If he or she is not able to do so, do it yourself. Check the journals in the field to see which publishers are advertising. Study the promotional materials that are mailed to you to see which new books have just been published. Talk with colleagues to get the benefit of their experience.

When you have identified three to five of the best-selling books, develop a competition matrix similar to the one shown in Box 13.3. Down the left-hand column, enter the subject of each chapter as you tentatively have conceptualized the book at Stage 2. Indicate with an x in which of your chapters each topic is treated. Then, show with the same symbol in which competing work that topic is emphasized.

Analyze the results carefully. Use the following questions to guide the review.

1. Does one of the competing works offer content that you now see should be in your own book? If so, change the table of contents.

2. Does your book present content not included in the competition's? If it duplicates too much of the competitions' content, editors will fault the proposal as simply another rehash.

Box 13.3 Competition Analysis

Component	Glatthorn	Hernandez	Walsh
Introduction	X	X	X
School violence history	X	X Very brief	
Cultural aspects: Japan, U.S., Costa Rica	X		
Incidence of violence	X	X	X
Causes	X		X
Dealing with the problem: Teacher training	X		X
Dealing with the problem: Student-centered programs	X	X	X
Dealing with the problem: Working with parents	X	X	X
Dealing with the problem: Security measures	X	X	X Brief treatment
A look ahead	X		
Resources			

3. Is the content of your book totally different from the competitions' content?

Most editors believe that your book should not make a radical departure from current conceptualizations in order to make the book seem attractive to more traditional professors. As an example, most forward-looking experts in teacher supervision now believe that a preobservation conference is not worth the time it takes. Yet a large group of supervisors still sees it as essential. When in doubt, include.

Submitting the Proposal

With such preparations made, you should be well prepared to submit a book proposal. You may wish to review those parts of Chapter 9 dealing with proposals.

WRITING THE BIG BOOK

Now you are ready to write. The discussion below takes you through the process step by step, but keep in mind that creativity cannot be programmed.

Getting the Basics Straight

Use 20-lb. paper. Double-space everything. Set your left-hand margin to 1½ or 2 inches. Do not use a justified right margin. All pages in the front matter should be numbered in Roman numerals; in the body of the manuscript, in Arabic numerals. Do not begin each chapter with page 1; instead, number consecutively. Some editors also ask you to put your name on each page. Thus, page 45 of the text would look like this:

Glatthorn, 45

WRITING THE FRONT MATTER

The *front matter* is publisher jargon for everything that comes before page 1 of your manuscript. The order in which these sections are explained below is generally the order in which they appear in the published book. Those that are asterisked are usually required by the publisher; the rest are optional.

Title Page. Choose a title that meets several criteria: It gives a clear sense of the book's focus, it is likely to attract readers, it appeals to the intended audience, and it does not sound like the titles of other books. Here are two examples of books on school violence. Which do you prefer?

A book on school violence for school administrators: *Making Your School Safe for Learning: A Handbook for School Leaders*

A book on school violence for professors: *Beyond Metal Detectors: School Violence in Perspective*

If the editor suggests another title, accept it, as long as it does not distort the actual content of the book. You should also include the following information on the title page: author's name, address, phone, fax, and e-mail address.

Table of Contents. Follow the suggestions given above in developing the content. It should appear right after the title page.

Foreword. This is an introduction to the work that frames the book as fulfilling a need. If you ask a leader in the field to write the foreword (a common practice), be sure to check with the acquisitions editor to learn the publisher's policy with respect to forewords written by someone other than the author. (And be sure to spell the word right: foreword.) If you do not include a foreword, then you need a preface or an introduction.

Preface/Introduction. These terms are used interchangeably to identify your preliminary comments. Placed after the foreword (if you use one) or after the table of contents, the preface is a valuable sales tool. It answers such questions as the following:

- Why did you write this book? What are your goals in writing the book?

- Why is its publication important at this time?

- How does this book differ from all the others? Do not use this section to criticize the competition. They are all good books; yours is just better.

- How is the book organized?

- What does each chapter contribute to the whole?

In writing the preface, you may use a more informal style. The following paragraph is an example of a style that might be used in the preface.

> Frankly, I wrote this book as a defensive manual, protecting myself against all educators who believe that more testing will improve our schools. And I wanted to share my defensive maneuvers with other teachers who also feel beleaguered by the testing menace. Just so that you are warned in advance, I take a stand: No more testing. All teachers who care about children should work in the most professional way to subvert this out-of-control movement.

You should consider whether the preface contains information that is essential in understanding the central thesis of the work. In that case, you might decide to place that content in Chapter 1.

Acknowledgments. Here you thank all those who assisted with this particular book: the publisher's editors, colleagues who helped, students, and funding agencies. As one editor put it, "The acknowledgments section is a public thank-you."

Dedication. This is a very brief personal statement that enables you to thank a long-suffering spouse, a professor who served as a mentor, or your mother for inspiring you to write.

WRITING THE REMAINING CHAPTERS

How you write the remaining chapters will, of course, be determined by your own writing habits and the book's content. However, I can offer some general guidelines derived from my experience and specific suggestions about the finer points of getting your book published.

General Guidelines

In what order should you write the chapters? Some experts suggest starting with the easiest chapter for you to write. Then move to the next easiest, and so on. That strategy seems to be effective if you have writer's block. However, the final product may seem disjointed and fragmentary. Writing the chapters in the order in which the chapters are listed in the table of contents makes it easier for you to produce a well-coordinated series of related chapters that conveys a sense of wholeness.

So you decide where to begin. Before you write, review your knowledge base, being sure that you have stayed on top of major findings in your field. Check the table of contents you developed to be sure the wording is the same as that used in the first page of the chapter. Also note the headings and subheadings used in the table of contents; they represent an outline of the chapter.

Write the chapter, correcting as you go. When you have finished the chapter, do a spell check and a grammar check. Then put the chapter aside, to let the chapter cook. When you are feeling fresh, read the chapter with a critical eye and note any changes you should make. Finally, ask a colleague to give the chapter a critical review.

Some Specific Suggestions

Several specific matters that often puzzle the writer are discussed in this section.

Use headings. Use headings liberally; they break up the page in a useful manner and help the reader track the chapter. Note two cautions here. First, the form of the headings should be consistent with that of a particular style manual, either one you have chosen or one recommended by your editor. Second, be sure the headings reflect the chapter organization. Some novice writers use headings capriciously, leaving the readers confused.

Use tables, figures, and boxes. A table uses columns and rows to display organized data. A figure is a sketch or a drawing used to illustrate a concept. A box is an organized collection of written information (a definition coined by the publisher of this work). Those visual representations make the reader's job easier and brighten the printed page. Usually, these visuals are set in special type. For that reason, they are handled in a special way.

In writing your manuscript, right after you first mention the table, figure, or box, refer the reader to it in this manner:

Figure 12.3 here

You then put the visual itself at the end of the chapter. By doing so, the editor will know where the table, figure, or box should appear on the printed page and will be able to handle the visual without interfering with the text itself.

Vary the wording of references. You can identify references in several ways, as shown by these examples:

Glatthorn (2000) argues that principals should be curriculum leaders.

As Glatthorn (2000) puts it . . .

Principals can play a vital role in curriculum (Glatthorn, 2000).

Principals can play a vital role in curriculum. (See especially Glatthorn, 2000.)

Several authorities in the field have recommended that principals should play a more active leadership role. (See, for example, Glatthorn, 2000; Jones, 2001; Young, 2002.)

Keep in mind two cautions. Ordinarily, you should not begin a sentence with the researcher's name; doing so gives him or her more importance than the reader expects. The only exception is if the name of the researcher is especially significant. The second caution is the need for variety. Specific forms used again and again soon become boring. You may wish to check one of the style manuals published for specific audiences.

TAKING CARE OF FINAL MATTERS

You are not quite finished. Four sections need special attention—the index, permissions, glossary, and author biography.

Index. Find out from your editor if you are expected to prepare an index, or whether that task is farmed out to a professional indexer. If you use a professional indexer, his or her fee will be paid out of your royalty account. My recommendation is to use a professional but to check his or her work carefully.

Permissions. Getting permissions is your job, not the publisher's. If you use another's work without permission, both you and the publisher are in trouble. Not everything requires permission, and copyright law is rather complicated. In general, authors of nonfiction works are governed by the following regulations as to the materials requiring permission:

1. More than 500 cumulative words from any nonfiction book

2. Any Internet or Web material

3. Interviews

4. More than 300 words from any single journal article or chapter

5. More than two sentences from a newspaper or magazine

Most publishers will supply you with permission request forms. Because getting permissions is a complicated and time-consuming process, you should start it as soon as you can. You may decide to use the services of the Copyright Clearance Center, which will handle all your permissions for a fee. (Their Internet address is www.copyright.com.)

Glossary. You may wish to prepare a separate glossary, especially if you have used several complex terms throughout the work. Here is an example of how a term should be defined.

Curriculum standard (sometimes referred to as "content standard"): A verbal statement of which content should be mastered by students in grades K-12, usually presented for each subject in the curriculum.

Notice that the definition begins with the broad category, similar in grammatical form to the term. Then, alternative forms are noted. Finally, the specific denotations are included. If your definition is a borrowed one, reference it. But do not write "According to Webster . . ." Instead, provide specific information about the dictionary used.

Author Biography. Your biography should be seen as an argument for buying the book, making clear why you are especially qualified, tailoring your biography to fit the book. Ordinarily, you would include any of the following items that establish your qualifications: present position, advanced degrees, special honors and awards, previous publications with the same publisher, and unique experiences. The biography should be 200 to 300 words. Title it "About the Author."

REVISING AND PREPARING FOR SUBMISSION

You have written and revised the entire book. What happens next? You read it through in its entirety, checking carefully for interchapter connections. Keep these questions in mind:

1. Does every reference in the text match the full reference in the reference list? For every item in the reference list, is there a mention in the chapter?

2. Does the numbering of tables, figures, and boxes match the visuals at the end of the chapter, and is the information correct?

3. Does the wording of chapter titles, as shown in the table of contents, match the wording of the chapter title on the first page of the chapter?

4. Is the page numbering correct? Often, the printer prints a blank page, which throws off the numbering system.

5. Are there mistakes in spelling, punctuation, and sentence structure that were not caught by the word processor checkers?

6. Are the interchapter references correct? When you first wrote Chapter 3, it was about security personnel in the school and you referred to it as Chapter 3. However, you have since revised the table of contents, and it is now Chapter 4.

This final revision is so important that you might ask a colleague to read it carefully to help catch last-minute mistakes. Check Chapter 8 for specific suggestions about revising your book.

Wrap It Up

Most publishers prefer that you send one disc and two hard copies of your manuscript. Send them by one of the overnight mail systems. Check with your editor to determine if he or she wants you to submit the manuscript electronically, an option that is becoming increasingly popular.

PROMOTING THE PUBLISHED BOOK

You probably thought you were finished when the author's copies arrived. You were wrong. The publisher expects you to help promote the book. Discuss with the acquisitions editor what the publisher expects authors to do.

You can use several professional methods. If you teach in a university, order your book as a basic or supplementary text, unless your university has a policy prohibiting this practice. The intent of such policies is to prevent professors from requiring students to buy the professor's book, when it is clearly not a quality work. Some writers-professors work out a compromise solution, such as giving students ordering information about the work; donating to a charity the funds generated by sales in their classes; or making the professor's book optional, not required.

Another effective promotional strategy is to sell the book at a consulting site where you are the workshop leader. Ethical issues again rise to the surface. If you are being paid to consult, some would argue that using that occasion to market your book is unprofessional. Some authors announce the publication through local media. This strategy seems to be effective in small towns. Finally, some authors have arranged with community bookstores to have a book signing.

The ethical issue of balancing your roles as salesperson and writer is one you have to resolve. Think it through, deciding the issue as a professional.

CHAPTER FOURTEEN

Using the Internet

As noted earlier in this book, the Internet has become one of the most essential writer's tools. But don't despair if you still have not joined the ranks of computer geeks. News reports tell us that William Bennett, prolific author, still uses a yellow pad and pencil for writing his books—and still does not use e-mail. So much for technology mandates.

But the Internet can be a big help to writers in ways that go beyond word processing. This chapter will help you understand what specific services are available and how best to use them. Two cautions are noted here. First, specifying a particular service does not usually constitute an endorsement or recommendation; it is mentioned here only as an example. At times, when I do recommend a specific service, I assure you that I have used it and found it satisfactory. Second, check all sources to be sure that they are still operating. One of the problems in the e-world is that information rapidly becomes obsolete.

In addition to this chapter, also review Chapter 5, which includes an extended discussion of using the Internet to build the knowledge base.

LEARNING FROM THE INTERNET

You can improve your writing by enrolling in an online writer's workshop. Some are sponsored by universities, some by professional writers' groups, and some by grassroots associations. For example, *Writer's Digest* (http://www.WritersOnLineWorkshops.com) sponsors workshops that offer participants a professional writer as a mentor, online teaching, and feedback about your writing. At the time of this writing, the workshops were offered at three skill levels: introductory, intermediate, and advanced. The only drawback of many writers' workshops is that most of them emphasize creative writing, with only occasional attention to nonfiction.

In choosing a workshop, get information about the following quality issues:

- Is the instructor a successful writer and teacher?

- Does the curriculum provide for different levels of learning?

- Are the topics covered ones where you need help?

- Are there opportunities for interaction with the instructor and other students?

- Is the sponsorship a stable and reliable organization?

SEEKING FUNDING

Because schools always seem to need additional funding, successful leaders know how to write effective proposals for funding—an activity that some call "writing grants." The Internet can greatly facilitate the identification of likely funding sources. For example, the Foundation Center (http://www.foundation.org) can put you in touch with more than 1,000 foundation Web sites. Chapter 19 of this book will give you more information about writing proposals for funding. Also, Peterson (2001) is an excellent guide for using the Internet to locate funding sources.

COMMUNICATING WITH OTHERS

E-mail helps you stay in touch with other writers and publishers. You can use e-mail to individuals and to groups. (The following discussion draws from several current sources, especially from Phillips & Yager, 1998.)

Individual E-Mail

You surely must know the advantages of e-mail to individuals. It is easy to use, inexpensive, and fast. It is so widely used that first-class "snail mail" has almost become obsolete. However, it does have a few drawbacks. First, it can be time-consuming, especially if you have subscribed to many services you really do not need. Many writers have found that they seem to waste a great deal of time responding to individuals whom they do not know and deleting "spam," or unsolicited junk mail that clutters up their e-mail in-box with sales pitches and other frivolous messages. The other problem is its difficulty establishing a paper trail for legal business.

Group E-Mail

If you wish to communicate with groups in chat rooms or forums, you have several options, but the process is a bit complex. First, you must subscribe to an automated Internet mailing list. One of the most often used is LISTSERV, although there are several others. The e-mail you receive from and respond to comes from a main computer, often one connected to a university mainframe. At the time of this writing, there were probably more than 70,000 electronic mailing lists, organized by subject. Two experts in the field (Phillips & Yager, 1998) recommend NeoSoft, a comprehensive list of mailing lists (http://www.neosoft.com). One other list to which you may wish to subscribe is the e-book list, available at http://www.greatcircle.com/majordomo/, which keeps users up-to-date about publishing books via the computer.

Once you have found the list you want, you inform the recipients that you wish to subscribe, using the same e-mail. Here is what you would write if you wanted to subscribe to the e-book list: subscribe e-book-list.

Some Problems With All E-Mail

Whether writing to individuals or groups, you will face two challenges. One is the relative lack of privacy, illustrated by this sad e-mail tale ("A Chief Is Criticized," 2001). The CEO of a large company sent a blistering e-mail message to all of his employees—one that made him look really bad. Someone leaked a copy to the Yahoo Web site, and from that point on, the foolish message was public knowledge. The *New York Times* reports that the company's stock dropped 22% over the next 3 days.

The other caution is to observe the special courtesies associated with all e-mail.

(The list is paraphrased from Phillips & Yager, 1998.)

- Do not use all capital letters. They are equivalent in e-talk to yelling.

- Avoid off-color jokes and language.

- Do not attack others by e-mail; it's called *flaming,* considered in bad taste.

- Lurk for a while before jumping in. *Lurking* is e-talk for reading group e-mail without contributing to the discussion. Lurk for a few weeks until you have a good feel for the neighborhood.

- Do not send spam; avoid commercials.

All this group e-mail can be helpful to novice writers: You have the opportunity to share your writing and get feedback; you make some e-friends who share your interest in writing; and you have a forum ready to hand, in which you can express your views about current issues. However, do not let chat rooms interfere with your writing. You don't get royalties from chat rooms.

PUBLISHING ON THE INTERNET

If you are having trouble getting published by a major publishing house, you might consider using Internet publishers. As noted by Vander Veer (2001), e-publishing has four types of operations, as follows.

1. *On-demand publishing* is a technological operation in which the technology enables a publisher to print just the number of copies

ordered. Thus, if you get orders this week for two copies of your book, the publisher prints two copies. If you get an order next month for one copy of your e-book, the publisher prints one copy.

2. *Content aggregation* is a process by which the publisher offers your book for a price using one of the commonly used formats. Purchasers can then access your manuscript by computer or handheld device.

3. *Electronic self-publishing* enables you to set up your own Web site as a means of publishing, promoting, and selling your book.

4. *E-zines* are electronic magazines. If you have an article that you would like to publish, consider sending it to an e-zine. One directory of e-zines is *E-Zines Today,* available at http://www.ezinestoday. com.

Taking a Closer Look

You can probably understand better the world of electronic publishing by taking a close look at the process. Suppose you have drafted a book on using handheld devices in schools to facilitate student learning, but you can't seem to convince a traditional publisher to publish it. You decide to send it to 1stBooks (http://www.1stBooks. com), one of many electronic publishers. They charge you a set-up fee of $159 and require you to send a $300 deposit. (Prices were current at the time of writing.) If they sell 1,000 or more copies of your book, your deposit is returned.

They proceed to publish your book. If you want them to promote your book, you pay an additional fee of $300 to $750.

Like most e-publishers, 1stBooks pays generous royalties: 100% for the first 300 copies, 40% thereafter, and 30% for print-on-demand books.

For unpublished authors, e-publishing can earn a modest profit. Do some arithmetic. You pay them $809 for publishing and promoting your book. It sells 60 copies, at $15 a copy. (Each family member buys 10 copies.) You get all the royalties, amounting to $900. You have earned $91, and you have a book published.

REFERENCES

A chief is criticized for sending a memo upbraiding employees. (2001, April 5). *New York Times,* p. C13.
Peterson, S. (2001). *The grantwriter's Internet companion.* Thousand Oaks, CA: Corwin.
Phillips, V., & Yager, C. (1998). *Writer's guide to Internet resources.* New York: Macmillan.
Vander Veer, E. A. (2001, March/April). Understanding e-publishing: A definitive treatment. *Writers' Journal,* pp. 15-16.

PART IV

Writing in Academic Settings

CHAPTER FIFTEEN

Writing the Review of the Literature

You may write a review of the literature for several reasons: to provide a basis for your own research, as part of a dissertation or a research report; to comply with the requirements of a graduate course; to provide a knowledge base for faculty problem solving; or simply to increase your own knowledge of a topic that interests you. In this chapter, you will find some general guidelines that apply to research reviews, followed by a discussion of the specific requirements for each purpose.

PLANNING THE REVIEW

The planning process is vital in writing a review. One process that has worked is presented in this section. The assumption here is that you have made a comprehensive retrieval of the literature and have made copies of all the articles you have found. How do you turn that pile into a sound review? That's the question answered in this and following sections.

Establish the Parameters of the Review

First, by drawing upon your experience and checking with your adviser (in the case of course papers, theses, and dissertations), establish the limits of your review. Answer these questions.

1. *What time period should be covered?* The answer, of course, depends on the nature of the review. If you were doing a historical study of retention/promotion, you might want to begin with the early practices used in the first graded schools. On the other hand, studies on the effects of computers on achievement might reasonably start with the 1970s, when the first serious studies were undertaken. For most educational studies, a time span of 1966 to the present should work. The ERIC database begins with 1966. Check with your adviser.

2. *How sharply focused should the review be?* The best strategy in answering this question is to write a problem statement and then use it to define the topical limits of your review. Here are two examples. Don Hagstrom and Susan Markle are both doing a study (in different institutions) of how computer use affects student motivation to learn. Don writes this problem statement:

Do computers make a difference?

That statement is so broad that he will have a database too broad—and probably too thin. Because the problem is so unfocused, he has accumulated a slush pile of sources covering such topics as the history of computers, changes in the hardware, computers' effects on achievement, and a few on student motivation.

In contrast, Susan poses the problem this way:

How does the use of computers in elementary and secondary schools affect student motivation to learn?

She limits her search and review to this problem statement and ends up with a sharply focused knowledge base that provides a sound foundation for her study. As a general rule, then, your literature review should be only as broad as the problem statement—and the narrower, the better. However, this issue is so crucial that graduate students should check with their advisers.

3. *What kinds of articles should be included?* In general, you should include three kinds of articles: empirical research (both qualitative and quantitative), research reviews, and meta-analyses of research. To apply this criterion, you have to know some crucial differ-

ences in what is often called *research*. This knowledge will help you make decisions about which sources to include.

• *Research.* Strictly speaking, the term *research* should be limited to systematic inquiry that is carefully designed to embody the principles of the scientific methods.

• *Review of Research* (sometimes termed *review of the literature*). This is a discussion of primary sources and their findings, all on the same topic. You will be writing a review of the research.

• *Meta-Analysis.* A meta-analysis uses statistical methods to synthesize several studies on the same topic that cover a span of years. A common measure, *effect size,* is used in order to make comparisons feasible.

You may decide to include articles that explain or critique a *theory.* A theory is a systematic analysis of concepts and their relationships used to explain or predict organizational or individual behavior.

Ordinarily, you should not include *reports of practice.* A report of practice is a description of what one individual or organization accomplished. Most reports of practice do not include empirical research or have not been systematically evaluated.

4. *How many references should be included?* There are three ways to answer this question. One sensible answer is, "Include all sources that fit within the parameters established and that meet standards of quality (discussed below)." Another answer is found by checking with the professor who assigned the paper. Although this question seems to annoy many faculty, you may decide to risk their displeasure because their expectations are so critical. Finally, you should find helpful these arbitrary minimums derived from experience. This is probably the weakest answer; use it only as a very general guide.

Nonfiction book: 100

Doctoral dissertation: 75

Master's thesis: 50

Course paper: 25

Box 15.1   Summary of Parameters

Problem: Student motivation to learn, K-12, influence of
   computers

Time Period: 1960–present

Focus: Narrow, problem-restricted

Types Included: Empirical research, reviews, meta-analyses

Number of References Expected: 40

Primary/Secondary: Primary only

Summary for school faculty: 15

5. *Should secondary sources be included?* If Munster publishes
an article about his study of motivation, that article is called a *primary
source.* If Smithers publishes an article in which he refers to the Munster study, then Smithers's article is a *secondary source.* In developing a review, use only primary resources.

When you have set these parameters, you probably will find it
helpful to summarize them in a form like the one shown in Box 15.1.

Select for Quality: Surface Markers

With the parameters established, you should evaluate all the articles for quality. You can first look for surface markers of quality,
which are indicators that can easily be identified. The first marker is
the reputation of the author. If you have done extensive reading in cooperative learning, you know that Robert Slavin is one of the leading
researchers in that field. The second marker is the journal that published the article. In general, research reported in research journals is
of higher quality than research published in journals aimed chiefly at
practitioners. The third marker is whether the journals submit articles
to external experts, who are called *referees.* Usually, articles reviewed

by referees are of higher quality than nonrefereed articles. You can determine if a journal is refereed by checking with research librarians. Finally, the date of publication is a useful marker. Generally, you should not refer to any article that is more than 10 years old unless it is a classic in the field or your adviser specifies differently.

Select for Quality: Intrinsic Markers

Once you have looked for the surface markers, you should next evaluate the quality of the research. Explaining all the complex statistics involved in research quality is beyond the scope of this work; however, some less complicated tests can be carried out by any intelligent person.

- *Does the author seems biased?* There are several ways you can check for author bias. Let's use as an example the phonics/whole language controversy. First, determine if the verbal language is slanted. Here is an excerpt from an article written by an author who favors whole language.

> The controversy involves more than research; it also involves one's view of the reading process. Does reading involve making exaggerated sounds and filling in the blanks—or is reading an exciting and creative work of the imagination that only big books can provide?

Another way to check for bias when two programs or views are being compared is to determine if the author includes approximately the same number of references for each side of the controversy. You can also check for bias by determining if the author has a vested interest in a particular program. For example, I have developed a curriculum model that is the primary basis for my consulting business. Any article I write about the model is very likely to be biased, even though I check carefully to ensure that I have given an unbiased account.

- *Does the author make claims not supported by the evidence?* The expectation in scholarly investigation is that all claims or assertions are supported with evidence. Unfortunately, some researchers make claims that represent their opinion and that are not supported with evidence or citations. Here is one example by a distinguished scholar culled from a quality journal.

> Character education programs are almost sure to fail their intended aims. They are ineffectual because they attempt to use schools to solve social problems that originate elsewhere (Alkanet, 2001, p. 16).

Now I happen to agree with Alkanet, but I should note that the first assertion ("almost sure to fail") would have been more persuasive if it had been supported by research evidence.

- *Does the author use questionable tests or measurements?* In some research, the investigator uses an inappropriate measure. Suppose, for example, that the author presents a writing program that purports to teach students "writing for real" and uses a test that assesses students' ability to write a standard "500-word theme." The test does not fit the program.

- *Does the author base claims on survey results with a low rate of return?* Getting people to complete and return surveys is rather difficult. As a consequence, some researchers claim too much when the rate of return is too small. Most expert researchers would like at least a 60% rate of return (Pyrczak, 1999). With a very low rate of return, you cannot be sure that those who did not respond feel the same as those who did.

Develop an Outline

With the selection process tentatively completed, you should develop an outline for your review. You can use either a deductive or an inductive process. In the deductive process, you reflect about all you have read and identify the big ideas and the order in which they should come. Here is an example of a brief outline on the topic of motivation that was developed deductively.

1. Definition and theories

2. Causal factors

3. Interventions: classroom climate

4. Interventions: curriculum

5. Interventions: instruction

The other organizing strategy is to use an inductive approach, in which the sources are grouped, as a means of identifying main ideas. You first review all sources you have marked with a "1," sorting them into related piles. Here, for example, are the piles that Walter Jordan made for his review of the literature on social promotion and retention and their effects on achievement. The topic is listed first, then the number of articles rated "1."

Definitions—1

Studies supporting social promotion—10

Studies supporting retention—3

Studies reporting no difference—2

Social promotion and retention and effects on self-esteem—4

Implications of findings—2

You then review the results to determine whether you need to revise the piles or do some additional searching. Jordan realizes that the articles on self-esteem should not be included and that he should try to find additional articles on the implications.

The next step using the inductive process is to make a tentative outline based on how you sorted and what you know about research reviews. Here is an outline based upon the promotion/retention sorting:

1. Introduction: purpose of the review

2. Search process

3. Definitions

4. Studies supporting social promotion

5. Studies supporting retention

6. Studies reporting no difference

7. Implications for practice

With either a deductive or an inductive process, you will probably want to include some sections that are obligatory, even though they may not appear as aspects of the topic. Observe that this is the nature of Topics 1, 2, and 3 above.

WRITING THE FIRST DRAFT OF THE REVIEW

With the outline at hand, you should be ready to write the first draft.

Write the Introductory Paragraph

The first paragraph will usually accomplish three goals: identify the research problem, state the purpose of the review, and provide an overview of the review. This paragraph shows one way of accomplishing these outcomes.

> This review of the literature focuses on the issue of whether retention or promotion has a more positive effect on the academic achievement of students in Grades 1-12. The purpose of such a review is to provide a scholarly foundation for the present study. The review begins by clarifying the parameters of the study and explaining the search-and-retrieval process. The body of the review is organized by the results of the study. A concluding section discusses the implications of the findings.

Explain the Search Process

The next section of the review usually explains the search process you used, including the parameters of the review.

> Before reviewing the results of this search, it would be helpful to review the search process. The review process began with a search of two databases, ERIC and Dissertations Abstract. The following parameters were set for the search: time frame, 1966; grades, K-12; descriptors, *motivation, computer, learning, research review.* Sources identified were subject to a quality check.

Only those studies meeting quality standards were selected for this report. The standards used are shown in Box 1.

Provide Definitions as Needed

You should provide definitions of key terms that are used in a special sense or that might not be known by readers. They can be placed at the end in a special section, or you may prefer to place the definitions at the beginning to aid comprehension. Here is an example.

Because it is important for two key terms to be understood at the outset, definitions are provided here. *Social promotion* is a policy of advancing students to the next grade, even though they have not achieved a specific standard. *Retention* is a policy of requiring students who have not met standards to repeat their present grade.

Certain points should be made about these definitions. First, define only the terms needed. Also, note the parallelism used here. Nouns are defined by nouns. For example, *retention,* a noun, is defined by the noun *policy.* If you decide to use a dictionary for the definition, provide full information about the reference. Do not write "According to Webster. . . ." Use the word *significant* only in the statistical sense; use instead synonyms such as *important* or *meaningful,* because the meanings can be easily confused.

Write the Sections in the Body of the Review

Now you should be ready to write the substantive paragraphs of the review. At this point, you might find it helpful to develop a more detailed outline for the topics identified. For example, here is a detailed outline for the topic "studies supporting social promotion."

Supporting Social Promotion

Early studies

Later studies

Exhibit 15.1. Example of Review

Chapter title, which does not appear here, is a level 1 head.

The term "left back" is a colloquial expression meaning "retained in grade."

Studies Supporting Social Promotion ——— *Level 2 Head*

Begins with generalization

The preponderance of well-designed studies support social promotion as a strategy for responding to the academic needs of low achievers. To support this assertion, the major studies will be examined in chronological order, followed by an analysis of reviews of the research. *indicates organizing plan*

Level 3 Head — Early Studies

Although early studies lacked the statistical sophistication of contemporary research, the researchers used the most valid research methods available to establish the academic effectiveness of social promotion.

Level 4 Head —— Studies Emphasizing Academic Gains.   Several of the studies conducted during the 1970s focused solely on academic achievement. One of the earliest studies was Watkins's (1967) research using a quasi-experimental design. He determined that fourth-grade students who were socially promoted scored higher on a mathematics/reading test than those who were retained. Using Watkins's research design, Armbruster (1972) achieved similar results.

Studies Including Self-Esteem.   A few of the early studies measured gains in both academic subjects and self-esteem.

Recent studies

Reviews of research

Note two points here. First, within each topical section, studies are ordered chronologically. Second, reviews of research are reported separately from the primary studies. In some instances, you may find it more appropriate to begin with the reviews of research. Actually, you can use many logical organizational principles, as long as they make sense and you make clear to the reader how you organized.

With the detailed outline in hand, you write the first section. Let's take an example and then analyze that to derive some guidelines you can use.

Be sure you write an interesting section that emphasizes the findings, not the researchers. Many dissertation writers commit the problem called "researcher-itis," which is simply listing the findings in random order. Here is an example of this problem.

Walker (1987) found no significant difference in achievement. Miller (1990) concluded that social promotion was better. Jurgens (1994) found that retention was better.

Close the Review

The reader expects that the review will close with a summary, especially at the end of long reviews. Consider this example:

This review indicates quite clearly that the promotion/retention controversy has had a long history. And that has been a troubled history of angry rhetoric and extreme claims. If a more dispassionate view is held, it would say something like this: If your only two choices are social promotion or retention, choose social promotion.

MEETING REQUIREMENTS OF SPECIAL USES

Each of the special purposes requires an understanding of its unique nature.

A Knowledge Base for Your Own Professional Growth

I have found it very useful to do a research review on an issue that seems to have continuing importance. I never know whether I will use these "for my eyes only" reviews, but from time to time, someone will call and ask, "What does the research say about. . . ." Because these reviews are for your eyes only, you need not worry about form. The only advice you need is to get the information for all references.

Here is a case in point. Before 1995, I used only APA4 documentation style. Among other specifications, it uses only the initials of the author's first and middle names. One morning, I received a call from the editor of one of the journals, asking me to do a piece on the teacher as a curriculum maker. The editor reminded me that his journal did not use APA4, so he needed first name and middle initial for all author references. I had to go back to the sources to find the first names of 36 authors. Now, I routinely copy the table of contents page, checking to be sure that it contains all the information I would need.

A Basis for Your Own Research

In writing a review of the research for your own scholarly investigation, your primary goal is to show how your study relates to existing knowledge. Does it confirm or contradict prior work? Does it extend existing knowledge? Does it suggest a new direction for future studies? In the dissertation, the answers to these questions would usually be found in Chapter 2. As part of your research article, a summary of existing knowledge is usually found in a separate section preceding an exposition of your methodology. In some contemporary approaches, you may decide to integrate the prior knowledge whenever you need to document an assertion.

These formal reviews are usually presented in a formal writing style—no colloquialisms ("kids") and no contractions ("you're"), careful documentation that follows an approved style guide, complex sentences, and longer paragraphs. Here is how such a style might sound.

In the first decade of this century, several experts in the field expressed concern that the voice of the classroom teacher was not being heard in the controversy about standards. (See especially Glatthorn & Fontana, 2000.) A few critics usually identified as conservative in ideology blamed classroom teachers as part of an educational establishment that resisted change and as a consequence should not be heard. When teachers' positions were expressed, the predominant attitude was one expressed by Walsh

(2000), "Standards are just one more fad we have to endure—sit this one out and it will go away" (p. 115).

A Response for a Graduate Course

Instructors of most graduate courses require a review of the research as a measure of the student's ability to synthesize the literature on a given topic. Although you should use a formal style, it may be somewhat less formal than the very formal style explained above. Thus, the first sentence in the paragraph above might be made just a bit simpler, like this. "Many experts noted that the voice of the teacher wasn't being heard in the standards controversy."

A Guide for Faculty Problem Solving

Faculty involved in solving a problem, such as "Should we put more emphasis on phonics in our reading instruction?" will usually develop better solutions if they have a sound knowledge base on the issue at hand.

Here, special organization and structure are needed. Study the communication processes your faculty uses. Most teachers want practical help. They ignore articles that repeat endlessly, "The research says. . . ." They are too busy to read more than one page. If these generalizations apply to the teachers you know, then you realize certain adaptations are essential if you are to reach them. Condense your review to a one-page handout. Use simple language. Put all references at the end. Use special formatting to make the handout easy to read. A sample handout on charter schools is shown in Box 15.2.

Box 15.2   Sample of Faculty Handout

Northside High School

Compiled by Ellen Jenkins   April 9, 2003

Self-Esteem: A Summary of the Research

1. *Does a person have one general sense of self—or several kinds of self-esteem?* Both. You have a general sense that, overall, you are a good person. But you know that, for example, you are not very good at basketball.

2. *Can I increase a student's self-esteem by praising him or her?* Probably not. Unearned praise is meaningless to students.

Reference

The following source was useful in compiling this review.

Appleby, S. M. (2001). The misuses of praise. *Educational Reviews, 56,* 265-270.

REFERENCE

Pyrczak, F. (1999). *Evaluating research in educational journals.* Los Angeles: Pyrczak Publishing.

CHAPTER SIXTEEN

Responding to Your Reading

Y ou always respond to your reading, at least in your thinking, if not in your writing. This chapter will help you write responses to your reading, for several audiences: yourself, to keep a record of your reading; your colleagues, to share information with them; and readers, who want to know if a book is worth buying.

BEFORE YOU READ

You need to take a few steps even before you read an article or book to which you will respond in writing. First, consider your audience. Also, reflect about your main purpose in writing: to amuse, to appreciate, to inform, to criticize, to share information. Finally, decide on the medium: your reading journal, a chat room on the Internet, a research journal, a practitioner journal, a memo to your colleagues. You may wish to make a brief note to yourself, like this one:

Audience: School administrators

Purpose: Help colleagues decide about reading a book

Medium: Practitioner journal

Reminders: Avoid jargon, emphasize positive, no references

Be sure to read four or five reviews in the journal for which you are reviewing. Pay special attention to their length, format, and content. Because those reviews have already been published, they can serve as models for your review.

READ APPRECIATIVELY AND CRITICALLY

With those decisions in mind, begin to read, both appreciatively and critically. Keep these criteria in mind as you read; they will help you make some sound judgments about the quality of an education book or article.

- *Provides Sound and Current Knowledge.* Two issues matter here. First, you expect your reading to offer sound information supported by research. Second, because the field of education changes so rapidly, the information should be current. You can approximate when the book or article was written by subtracting from the publishing date 1 year for articles and 2 years for books.

- *Demonstrates a Deep and Comprehensive Knowledge of the Field.* What else has the author written? Does the author have credibility in his or her field? This does not rule out younger writers; it simply raises a caution about instant experts.

- *Avoids Bias.* All of us are biased about some educational issues. I am biased against "brain-compatible learning" when it stretches scientific knowledge so far that it might break. The point is that the best authors admit their biases and take special pains to hold them in check. Here are some ways to check for excessive bias. Does the author . . .

    1. Have the same number of references for both sides of a controversy?

    2. Acknowledge models and methods other than his or her own?

    3. Recognize that education issues rarely have simple or single answers?

    4. Use objective language?

- *Provides Sufficient Support for Assertions.* Contrast these examples:

Not Supported: Social promotion has failed as an educational strategy.

Supported: Three major studies have concluded that students who were socially promoted earned better scores on high-stakes tests than those who were retained. (See Stokes, 2000; Thompson, 1998; Waller, 1999.)

- *Organizes Clearly.* Check the table of contents. Is there some system to the way chapters are ordered, or does the order seem hit-or-miss? Is each chapter organized clearly, with appropriate headings?

Read carefully, taking notes as you read. You should, of course, read in your own style. Here is a process that you might find effective.

1. Skim the article or book to get a general idea of its content.

2. Read with both an appreciative and a critical attitude. To read appreciatively is to be sensitive to and aware of the positive aspects of what you are reading. To read critically is to read with an eye for weaknesses.

3. Take notes as you read. Here is an example:

   The Weak Teacher

   Positive

   p. 34. Good forms—useful in dismissal

   Negative

   p. 36. Narrow view of observing

WRITE YOUR RESPONSE

Now you should be ready to write. The content and order of each type vary so much that each needs to be examined separately.

Your Reading Journal

Many educators keep a reading journal. Such a record of reading serves many purposes: It shows how your tastes have changed, shows how educational trends have changed, reminds you of what you have read (so you don't buy a book you have read), and suggests books that are worth rereading.

Because the reader's journal is a highly personal medium, there is only one rule: Keep it honest. Don't fake your personal response. The following is an example from a teacher's reading journal, just to show how one person responded.

> 6/15. *Coping With Standards*. Good to hear teachers' voices for a change. Surprised these teachers are so accepting of standards. Gives a very general picture of national trends. Needs more detail here, more statistics.

Memo to Faculty

School administrators should, from time to time, let faculty know about books and articles worth reading. Such a practice raises the general level of faculty discourse, keeps faculty informed, and helps create a positive image of the administrator. Keep in mind some simple guidelines: keep it brief, stress the positive, and avoid an avuncular tone. This example shows one approach.

> Current issue of *Kappan* focuses on middle school—many fine articles. I especially liked Hopping's article on "multiage teaming"—practical, research-based. If you'd like to read and discuss it, let me know.

This brief note has some desirable features. It emphasizes the positive, calls attention to a strength of the work, and offers follow-up activities.

The Capsule Review

The capsule review is a brief (100 to 200 words) review of a current book. Consider this example, noting its distinguishing features.

The Weak Teacher (2003). (Philadelphia, ProBooks). W. A. Thomas.

Written for school administrators who have weak teachers on their hands, this book takes them through the dismissal process in step-by-step fashion. The book should be of help to those principals who often make major mistakes in the dismissal process; there is a sample letter for each step in the process.

The strengths of the book are clear. It gives specific advice about what can often be a messy process. The major weakness of this book is the lack of a research base; only two references are provided—both refer to publications by the authors of the present work. One other concern is the weakness in its treatment of how to strengthen the weak teacher.

This is a book from which novice principals would profit; experienced principals do not need it.

These features are noteworthy. It provides information about the title, author, year of publication, and publisher. It identifies the audience and summarizes the content. Then it notes major strengths and weaknesses, concluding with a recommendation.

The Full Review

You may be asked by one of your professors to write a detailed critique of an assigned reading, or you may be asked by the editor of a journal to review a current work. Such full reviews may be of several different types, as follows.

- Review of one book, emphasizing content of the work. These reviews are chiefly intended to give readers information about the content so that they decide whether to buy.

- Review of one book, chiefly to criticize or praise the work, for readers who want to know the strengths and weaknesses of a current work

- A comprehensive review of one book, balancing content, evaluation, and recommendation

- Review of two or three new books on a topic of current interest, to make comparisons or synthesize findings. For example, you might decide to do a critique of three "brain-based learning" books.

Each of these reviews has different requirements. Because the balanced, comprehensive review of one book best demonstrates the key guidelines, the following discussion focuses on that type.

Identify the book. At the top of the first page, put the identifying information: title, copyright date, author, place of publication, and publisher.

Begin effectively. Begin by using an effective strategy. Here are some ways to begin.

- *Begin with an assessment:* "Michael Fullan's new edition on the change process is one of those 'must-have' books for educational leaders."

- *Begin with some general background:* "The 'teacher bashing' continues unabated, after 20 years of complaining about teachers. Now a very fine book . . ."

- *Begin with a brief note about the author:* "For many years now, Michael Fullan has been recognized as the guru of the change process."

There are, of course, several other openings. Just remember that your goal is to snare the reader.

Use a clear organizing principle. Consider this simple outline:

Introduction (as above)

Summary of Content

Strengths of the Book

Exhibit 16.1 Sample Full Review

(Note: The book reviewed here is a real book; the identifying information has been omitted to avoid embarrassing the authors and the publisher.)

One of the most difficult tasks of first-year principals is staff evaluation. The difficulty is exacerbated when weak teachers are being evaluated for tenure and contract renewal. The process must be professionally effective, completely legal, and totally equitable. This book should help principals avoid the many pitfalls that face them in evaluating weak teachers.

THE BOOK'S CONTENT

This eight-chapter work seems to have three major divisions, although the table of contents is not organized in this manner. The first section is preparing for the evaluation, including a chapter on the nature of the weak teacher and one on establishing the evaluation process. The middle three chapters explain the process itself. The concluding section deals with the dismissal process and the third-party hearing.

STRENGTHS OF THE WORK

The book's chief strength is its specificity. Each chapter is organized clearly and provides very specific guidance. Consider, for example, Chapter 2, establishing the evaluation process—a two-page chapter. It begins by suggesting a time line, August. It then suggests nine procedures that should occur in August. The last procedure is to orient new students, although it does not indicate how doing so will help the evaluation process. The chapter ends by providing two form letters, one welcoming teachers and one assigning mentors. Other chapters are similar in format and organization.   *(continued)*

Exhibit 16.1 Sample Full Review (continued)

WEAKNESSES OF THE BOOK

The major weakness of the book is its lack of professional substance. Most chapters list many suggestions without explaining the rationale, making reference to the research, or offering details of the suggestions. Consider the chapter on identifying weak teachers—a critical and complex procedure. It suggests 34 procedures that should occur in October. Some of these are professionally sound: "Hold a preevaluation conference." Some seem foolish: "Take pictures in the classroom." A few are professionally questionable: "Refer the teacher to the weekly bulletin."

A related flaw in the book is the absence of good research. Here is the compelling evidence for this criticism: The reference list for the entire book has only two items, which just happen to have been written by authors of the present work.

RECOMMENDATION

New and aspiring principals who like specific guidance should find much here to assist them. Old hands who want to read the best in current thought about weak teachers should seek out other works, starting with Edwin Bridges.

Weaknesses of the Book ("strengths" and "weaknesses" may be reversed)

Recommendation

Observe that you may alter the order of the book's strengths and weaknesses. Consider such factors as the overall assessment and the relative importance of the two topics. Also, special formatting will help, as the model review in Exhibit 16.1 indicates. Read the sample review both appreciatively and critically.

CHAPTER SEVENTEEN

Mastering the Academic Style: Research Proposal, Thesis, and Dissertation

The research proposal, the master's thesis, and the doctoral dissertation are different in length, timing, and complexity. However, they are alike in the writing style expected. With all three, you are expected to use the academic style. This chapter takes a close look at that style as it plays out in the three types of writing. Those who wish to learn about the entire dissertation process should read a current book on the subject, including my own *Writing the Winning Dissertation* (published by Corwin Press).

WRITING THE ACADEMIC STYLE: ORGANIZATION

The organization of these three types has crystallized into a formulaic order, with the three types distinguished from each other only in minor ways.

Research Proposal

In most universities offering advanced degrees, the proposal for the thesis or the dissertation is defined as the first three chapters of the master's thesis or doctoral dissertation. Those chapters and their typical content are as follows:

Chapter 1: Introduction to the study: statement of the problem, significance of the problem, overview of the methodology

Chapter 2: Review of the literature relating to the research problem: organized by topic

Chapter 3: Methodology: general research type, site of study and access to site, participants in the study, data collection and analysis, instruments

However, some universities have accepted alternative forms. First, some accept a "working proposal," a condensed form of the proposal. Some argue that in doing action research or ethnography, the working proposal offers greater flexibility; the problem and the methods tend to emerge as the study gets under way. A second change is to integrate the literature review. Rather than writing a separate chapter, the author places it wherever it seems appropriate.

Organization of the Thesis and Dissertation

Most universities prefer the traditional five-chapter format. The first three chapters are those noted as for the proposal. In addition, two chapters complete the research report.

Chapter 4: Results of the study, usually presented according to the research questions

Chapter 5: Summary and discussion. Some faculty prefer using "Conclusions and Recommendations" for the final chapter. About this and all other matters of style, check with your adviser.

Some faculties propose a simpler organization. The first chapter introduces the study; the final chapter presents the summary and discussion. The intervening chapters may be in any order that is clear to the reader.

MAKING THE ORGANIZATION CLEAR

Two related methods can be used to make the organization clear to the reader.

Use Verbal Signals

You can use several verbal signals. First, in the opening paragraph of each chapter, provide an overview of what is to come. Consider this example, the opening paragraph in Chapter 1.

> This dissertation reports the research on the correlation between teachers' absences and student achievement in mathematics. This chapter identifies the research problem of the study, discusses the importance of the problem, describes the context of the study, and presents an overview of the dissertation.

Think of that paragraph as a commitment to the reader. Upon reading that first paragraph, the reader expects to find the content as specified.

You can also achieve clarity by putting the topic sentence first in the paragraph. As you may remember from previous discussions, the topic sentence is one that states the main idea of the paragraph. Here is an example of the first sentence of the chapter on the importance of the teacher absence study.

> The issue of teacher absence and its influence on achievement has real importance at this time. As those absences tend to increase…

Use Appropriate Headings

The correct use of headings can be a great aid to making the organization clear. The first thing you have to decide is the number of lev-

Exhibit 17.1 Four-Level Headings

Level 1	2. REVIEW OF LITERATURE

The issue of the effects of social promotion and retention of students not achieving at the expected performance standard has been intensively studied for at least 60
years. In order to provide a useful context for the present
study, this chapter reviews the most influential of those
studies, presenting first those studies supporting social
promotion and then those supporting retention.

Level 2   Studies Supporting Social Promotion

In general, most of the studies report several benefits
of social promotion.

Level 3   Impact on Self-Image

Since Lawson's 1937 study, there have been 21
research reports concluding that social promotion has
a positive effect on the self-image of elementary
students.

Level 4   Early studies. The early studies, those made in the
30 years following Lawson's study, were poorly
designed.

els that chapter will have. Study Exhibit 17.1, which shows how a
four-level heading works.

Note several distinguishing features. First, it follows the recommendations of APA5. Second, it has four levels: Level 1, for the chapter title; Level 2 for the main headings, used for the major divisions of
the chapter; Level 3, for the subdivisions of the main divisions; and
Level 4, for the divisions of Level 3. Each level is different in several
ways: underlining or no underlining; capitalization or caps and lower
case; flush left or indented; period after the heading or no period.
Four levels should work in most research reports. If you need three or
five levels, check the details in APA5.

CHOOSING THE RIGHT WORDS

Use words that sound formal and objective. Here are some specific guidelines.

1. *Minimize references to yourself.* If you need to refer to yourself, you have three choices.

- Use "this researcher": This researcher then interviewed three principals.

- Use first-person pronouns, "I," "me," "my": I then interviewed the three principals.

- Use the passive: The principals were then interviewed.

I prefer the first person, "I," but some professors believe it is too informal.

2. *Avoid colloquialisms.* A colloquialism is an informal expression that is quite acceptable in informal speaking and writing but is considered inappropriate when the formal style is expected. Check the list shown in Box 17.1.

3. *Avoid clichés* (pronounced klee-SHAYZE). A cliché is an overused expression, such as "systemic," "paradigm shift," or "middle school concept."

MASTERING SENTENCES

The optimal structure of the English sentence is a complex matter that is difficult and perhaps misleading to reduce to a general formula. If you continue to make sentence structure errors, you need a good editor who can give you individual help.

To understand English sentences, you need to understand some basics of grammar. *Clauses* are groups of words containing subjects and verbs. English has two types of clauses: An independent (or main) clause can stand alone, but a dependent (or subordinate) clause

Box 17.1   Using Formal Expressions

Avoid Using	*Instead Use*
A lot	Many
OK	Satisfactory
Isn't (and other contractions)	Is not
Exam	Examination
PE	Physical education
TV	Television
Kids	Students or children

cannot. Those two types of clauses can be used to describe four kinds of sentences: simple, compound, complex, and compound-complex (see Box 17.2).

There are no hard and fast rules about using the four types. However, the following guidelines—with examples—may help you write the formal style.

1. *Use chiefly complex sentences.*

According to several studies, boys who watched more than 25 hours a week of television became more aggressive as adolescents.

2. *Use compound-complex sentences sparingly.* They tend to get too long but can provide some variety.

Although some sociologists do not believe that analyzing the causes of violence is useful, the culture is one obvious factor; it is clear that some cultures are more violent than others.

3. *Avoid using compound sentences.* Overuse of the compound suggests a childish style. Use the compound only when the two main clauses are of equal importance, as in this example:

Box 17.2   Kinds of Sentences

Types of Sentence	Number of Main	Number of Subordinate
Simple	1	0
Compound	2	0
Complex	1	1+
Compound-complex	2	1+

The girls had a mean score of 7.3; the boys had a lower score of 6.4.

This example illustrates an inappropriate use:

I interviewed the principals; then I asked them to compete the survey.

That sentence would be improved by changing it into a complex sentence, like this one:

After I interviewed the principals, I then asked them to complete the survey.

One way of checking for overuse of the compound sentence is to watch for "and" when it is used to join clauses. If it is used to join nouns, verbs, adjectives, or adverbs, there is no problem, as these examples illustrate.

We surveyed all teachers and students. (Two nouns)

We conducted interviews and administered surveys. (Two verbs)

The trouble comes when you spot an "and" connecting two clauses, like this example:

The teachers notify the principal, and the principal notifies the parent.

This next example is much improved:

The teachers notify the principal, who in turn notifies the parents.

4. *Use simple sentences sparingly.* A simple sentence can be used for variety or special emphasis, as in this one:

They all failed the test.

5. *Avoid the mistake of dangling elements.* To state it more simply, if you begin with a phrase that has an implied subject, start the main clause with the subject. Here is a correct example.

After scoring the test, I provided remediation to those who failed.

This next sentence is wrong.

After scoring the test, remediation was provided.

Why is it wrong? The implied subject of the first phrase is "I," not "remediation."

6. *Avoid placing any elements between the subject and its verb.* The basic word order in English is subject-verb-object. If you wish to add elements, place them before the subject-verb-object or after the s-v-o. Here are illustrations of this guideline:

To my amazement, all the boys passed the test.

All the boys passed the test, to my amazement.

Here is an ineffective example:

All the boys, to my amazement, passed the test.

7. *Avoid beginning too many sentences with the name of the researcher, unless the name is important.* As explained elsewhere, beginning with the researcher's name gives too much emphasis to it. Here is an effective example:

> Self-esteem can best be raised through earned achievement (Booker, 2001).

This next example shows an ineffective use:

> Booker (2001) determined that self-esteem is raised by earned achievement.

MASTERING THE PARAGRAPH

In writing academic prose, you need to keep in mind just a few reminders. First, use longer paragraphs, a hallmark of academic writing. Rather than counting words, consider the appearance of paragraphs on a word-processed page of manuscript. If you have a string of short paragraphs, the page has an immature look. On the other hand, if there is only one long, unbroken paragraph, the page looks dull. As a general rule, check to see if you have two or three paragraphs to a manuscript page. If you have only one long paragraph, break it up into two. If you have more than three, consider developing each short paragraph more fully.

In considering this matter of paragraph length, do not be misled by the short paragraphs you may find in some journals. The writer probably wrote longer paragraphs, but the editor divided them into shorter ones. This division makes the page look more interesting. The other reason that writers use shorter paragraphs is that the shorter ones work especially well in a book (like this one) that explains a process. Long sentences and paragraphs can get confusing.

As noted previously, topic sentences help readers comprehend the main idea of a longer paragraph. A topic sentence is a sentence that states the main idea; it is usually expressed at a higher level of generality than what follows. To see how this kind of sentence functions, compare these two paragraphs.

Principals seem to be reluctant to share power with teachers. They perceive power as a limited commodity. They also worry that school-based decision making will mean increased responsibility for them, because school-based management requires that the principal and staff make decisions about budget, schedules, and staffing. Finally, they wonder if teachers have the necessary leadership skills to warrant involving them in identifying and solving problems.

Now see how the topic sentence brings those elements together.

For several reasons, principals seem reluctant to embrace site-based management and shared decision making. Principals seem to be reluctant to share power with teachers. They perceive power as a limited commodity. They also worry that school-based decision making will mean increased responsibility for them, because school-based management requires that the principal and staff make decisions about budget, schedules, and staffing. Finally, they wonder if teachers have the necessary leadership skills to solve problems.

SOME FINAL REMINDERS

Here is a list of reminders about using academic prose, derived chiefly from my experience in chairing approximately 140 dissertations.

1. Everyone needs a good editor, someone skilled in editing the academic style. Hire a good one, acknowledging his or her assistance.

2. If any of this advice seems in conflict with your adviser's, the adviser is always right.

3. This book you are now reading is not presented as a model of the academic style. In several places, I have ignored the advice given here in order to achieve greater clarity and interest. If you need models of the academic style, read scholarly books and articles.

4. The pronoun *we* is an ambiguous one. Does it mean the author? Does it mean a group of people? Or does it stand for educators in general? Because of this ambiguity, avoid using it in academic prose.

5. The word *data* was always considered a plural (of the singular *datum*). Thus, careful writers would write "The data suggest. . . ." Now, many dictionaries note that it can be a singular or a plural. Use it as a plural, the conservative choice.

PART V

Writing in the Organization

CHAPTER EIGHTEEN

Publishing in the Local Paper

Sharon Schlegel and Allan Glatthorn

There's nothing wrong with blowing your own horn, especially when you believe that building support in the local community is a vital aspect of leadership. However, you have to do so with a little modesty and much panache. This chapter helps you learn how to get published in the local paper. Note that in this instance, "getting published" includes what might be termed "indirect publishing," where you suggest stories and assist reporters in writing stories. In such a case, you haven't written a thing, but you deserve credit for getting favorable publicity.

CULTIVATING LOCAL SOURCES

Successful educational leaders have their roots in the community— even if those roots are shallow ones. Effective educators work with community leaders without getting deeply involved in political controversy. They involve parents in school matters. They join the local service club to get to know the movers and shakers. They appear at public events. And they take the time to build relationships with the local press. They develop relationships built on trust. Local journalists know that those local educators can be trusted to tell the truth, even if the truth may be damaging in the short run. They make special efforts to learn the needs of the media. Thus, when they speak, the public listens.

ESTABLISHING CONTACT

Even before you have written a word, you need to make some preparations, first by establishing contact and then by studying the local paper. You should establish contact by calling the city editor or managing editor for the names of the following:

1. The person covering your school district and to whom he or she reports

2. The community news editor

3. The feature editor

4. The education editor

5. The staff member who should be your primary contact

Call your contact once, early in the school year, just to introduce yourself and offer to help in any way. Your goal is to establish a working relationship with the press.

At the same time you are establishing contact, you should study the local paper. Learn which sections are contained in the paper and which types of articles are published in each section. For example, if the story is community-centered (the Garden Club of the town annually volunteers to sell hot dogs at the football games), find out if the paper has a community news editor who would like such a feature. If your article is centered on one person (a principal who started an after-school motorcycle repair club), then call the features editor. If you want to tell the story of a school athlete who has overcome a physical handicap, then contact the sports editor. Or if you find a columnist who writes human interest stories, then contact him or her with some idea.

You can get published with four kinds of writing for the local paper: a news release, a letter to the editor, a feature story, and a column

---

Box 18.1   News Release Form

NEWS RELEASE

CONTACT: Lester James   FOR RELEASE: October 10, 2004
            PHONE: 252 396 2345
            FAX: 252 396 2344
            E-MAIL: James@pub.com

LOCAL PRINCIPAL HONORED

---

of your own. In most cases, of course, how much the paper accepts of your writing depends on the size of the paper, their own staff, and the quality of your work.

WRITING THE NEWS RELEASE

The news release, a news story prepared by the sending organization, is an effective way to get published in the local paper. Many school systems have a public relations department that handles all official releases. If your organization has such an office, be sure to work with them. The first step in writing the release is to use a standard heading. Box 18.1 shows one heading that contains all the needed information.

Then write the news story itself. News stories begin with a lead paragraph that tells the most important aspect of the story.

Here is an example of a good lead:

John Smith, principal of North High School, has been chosen as "Principal of the Year" for the state of North Carolina. Smith was one of 25 nominees competing for the award.

Here is how a novice might begin the same story:

The "Principal of the Year" committee met last night at the high school to choose the principal to be honored. The meeting was chaired by Walter Thompson.

With a good lead to catch the reader's interest, you then follow with the next most important piece of information, and so on until the end, where you place the least important information. Placing the less important material at the end of the release makes it easy for the editor to cut the story if space requires it.

The second paragraph might start this way:

Smith is known locally for his success in turning around North High School, where student achievement went from last in the state last year to fifteenth this year, as measured by state tests.

The story might end with this note:

Smith has been principal at North for 2 years. He lives with his wife and two children at Parker's Falls.

In addition to this special organization, news stories have other distinguishing traits. Keep these points in mind when you write news releases.

1. *Use short paragraphs—no more than 75 words.* Long paragraphs in the newspaper do not look interesting.

2. *Quote the people involved.* Quotations help increase reader appeal.

3. *Keep the story objective.* If you feel you must praise someone, do so in a quotation, as in this example.

Jennie Hawkins, history teacher, had this to say about Smith: "He really deserved the award—he makes us all want to work harder."

4. *Do not use titles—no Dr., Mr., Ms.* If you think your readers have to know that you have the degree, be a bit subtle: "Smith received his doctorate from East Carolina University."

5. *Keep news stories short.* They should be no more than five brief paragraphs and no more than one page.

Exhibit 18.1 Example of Letter to the Editor

I would like to congratulate the Wilson High School girls' lacrosse team, which just completed a perfect season. Even in the absence of team leader Gwen Jackson, out with a sprained ankle, our team defeated Roosevelt High 5-0 last week to close the school's only no-loss season. I especially wish to praise Coach Walt Jameson, who used his considerable experience in guiding the team to victory. We wish the team well as they prepare for the state tournament.

—John Smith, Principal, Wilson High School

WRITING LETTERS TO THE EDITOR

In writing a letter to the editor, keep in mind several cautions. Once published, the letter becomes part of an archive. It has permanence; readers can read it again. These features mean that you should avoid certain traps. Do not deal with political issues or attack public figures. Do not inject religion into current issues. And most of all, do not get into public battles with the media. They almost always have the last word.

These admonitions do not mean that as an educational leader, you give up your First Amendment rights. In fact, in serving as a role model for children and youth, you should demonstrate the courage of your convictions, without alienating the public you serve. Exhibit 18.1 shows a sample letter that is short and positive, calling attention to student achievement in athletics. Be sure not to overdo such letters. They quickly get tiresome.

WRITING FEATURE ARTICLES

A feature article usually presents the human side of the news. These examples illustrate the kinds of features you might write or have a reporter write.

- An unusual extracurricular activity, such as the radio club

- A student with disabilities who has achieved much despite the challenges

- A faculty member with an interesting background

- An interesting member of the noncertified staff, such as a maintenance worker working toward her master's degree

WORKING WITH A REPORTER OR JOURNALIST

Because most features are staff written, you probably will find yourself using the indirect approach of working with a member of the newspaper staff. But don't lose credibility by becoming a pest. Do not fax or call more than once every 4 to 6 weeks to suggest feature ideas. Present two or three story ideas at a time. Fax a rundown of the ideas to the paper, with "Attention" to the appropriate reporter or editor. Then call or write a few days later if you haven't heard anything, to inquire as to the response. Your letter to the editor or features writer might look like this:

Here are some ideas for possible features I thought you might want to know about. I'll be in touch in a few days to see what you think.

(1) the teacher who spends summers working with the homeless (and has for 8 years now)

(2) teachers who left other professions for teaching (We have a former actor, a former stockbroker, and a former nationally recognized athlete.)

(3) why we continue to teach Latin—who takes it and why

If any of these should appeal to you, let's talk soon about how I can help you develop them and put you in touch with the right people. I will check back in the near future.

Remember, always fax or write first. Reporters make and get dozens of calls a day. Proceeding in this manner gives the reporter a chance to think over or develop an interest. Then, if he or she hasn't called in 4 days, reinforce with a call. The journalist may have forgotten all about your suggestions and would welcome the reminder. Make sure you've first gotten permission from the story's subject— and in the case of a student, the student's family.

If your ideas are rejected, take the rejection graciously. If a reporter immediately passes on an idea, ask if he or she thinks it might work somewhere else in the paper, and whom you should contact. If "no" is again the response, move on. If the reporter or editor likes the idea, be prepared to give him or her names of the educators to call, their phone numbers, and the times most convenient. Ask about photos, gently suggesting one or two options, and offer to help set them up. Never ask to see the story in advance of publication. This is prohibited at almost all newspapers. However, if the story is controversial, you may ask if the reporter would mind reading back specific quotations. If the answer is "no," accept that, if you have confidence in the paper's integrity. If the reporter/editor likes your idea but isn't ready to proceed, ask when you can send the names and numbers of those to contact. If you hear nothing within that time frame, call again.

WRITING THE FEATURE YOURSELF

If you are working with a very small or weekly paper, inquire as to whether they will accept features you write, what they want in terms of length and format, and whether you can supply photos.

Should they agree, send your story by e-mail, fax, or hand (a nice way to further establish contact). Unless the story is not timely, do not use regular mail. If you include photos, attach a caption and indicate if the photo needs to be returned. Offer to pick it up, if you can, or include a return envelope.

Finally, try to develop a nose for news that lends itself to a feature. If the principal gets an award, that's an announcement for the local news section. If it's a national award, that's a news story. If he used to be a carpenter, came to teaching in his 40s, and now says all principals and all teachers should work in a different profession first, that could be worth a feature interview or profile.

And keep trying, no matter how often you get a "no." Ask your contact what you're doing wrong if you never get a positive response.

Exhibit 18.2 Example of Feature Article

Tim Washington, a local teacher, won't be vacationing or studying this summer. Instead, he'll be working full-time at Eagles Wings, a soup kitchen for the homeless. Tim teaches physics at Central High, where he is known for his success with low achievers. Then why is he working at the soup kitchen? He answers with a tone of quiet confidence.

"When my grandfather and grandmother first came to town with their five children, the soup kitchen was the first to help them survive, until Granddad could find a job. And I believe in paying back. Besides, it's cool down there." He chuckled as he prepared for his fifth-period advanced physics class.

We met Tim in his spotlessly clean physics lab. All the lab equipment had been carefully placed, probably reflecting his 20 years in the marines.

Sitting on a student desk with his long legs dangling, he explains slowly and carefully what his soup kitchen tasks are, as if he is explaining the speed of light.

"It all depends on what they need done. Usually, I serve the folks there, then clean up when they have finished. Sometimes I cook. And at least once a week, I settle arguments between our guests. The arguments are usually about food." He smiled.

When asked if he missed taking summer courses, he seemed to become just a bit defensive. "I stay up-to-date in other ways," he said. "And every day in the soup kitchen, I am learning a lot about human nature."

The press want local stories, and if you're pleasant and not pushy, they should be eager to hear from you and work with you.

There is no formula for features because they differ so much. Exhibit 18.2 illustrates some common characteristics. (Only part of the feature is presented in the exhibit.) First, features begin with a sentence or two that should catch the reader's attention. Do not begin with a newsy lead. Second, a few descriptive details of the subject's appearance are integrated with the rest of the content, just to help the readers imagine the subject. Also, quotations are used extensively. If the subject of the interview speaks with a pronounced dialect, do not try to imitate it in writing. Doing so usually comes across as patronizing or ridiculing. Finally, the setting is described briefly, to provide a context for the feature.

WRITING A COLUMN

Once you have established a good working relationship with the local paper, you may wish to discuss with the editor the possibility of your writing a monthly educational column for the paper. In presenting your proposal to the editor, make the argument that an educational column would be good for the paper for reasons such as the following: It would offer an advantage over the competition (if there is a competing paper), it would attract subscribers who have children in the local schools, and it would cast a positive light on the newspaper in its role as the voice of the community.

Here are some of the conditions you might wish to specify. First, you would discuss community educational concerns; the column would not be a "puff piece" for local schools. Second, you would deliver the column 1 week before the paper's deadline. Finally, you would accept compensation at the level the paper would pay a fledgling reporter.

Now I must confess that I have tried, with no success, to sell the column idea to our local paper. I hope that you have better luck than I.

CHAPTER NINETEEN

Writing Successful Proposals for Funding

O ne of your roles as a leader is to seek special funding. Even in hard times, special funds are available from government agencies and foundations. This chapter will take you through a step-by-step process in writing an effective proposal.

BEFORE YOU START WRITING

Certain preparations will help you get off to a good start.

Marshal Your Resources

You will need to acquire or borrow some special resources. The resource list at the end of this chapter gives you basic information about several funding guides that list funding agencies. Check with the nearest university library to find out which of these guides is available. Note that some provide for online searches.

By reviewing these reference guides, identify three that are up-to-date, comprehensive, and easy to use. Use these source books to identify three likely funding sources. Use your computer to build your own database. For each likely funding source, enter this information:

- Name of source, name of contact, address, phone, and e-mail address

---

Box 19.1   Sample Preliminary Contact Letter

I write to request a half-hour conference with you in your office for the purpose of learning more about your foundation and its funding priorities.

We are a rural school system that serves very scattered towns, with large numbers of unemployed. Despite these obstacles, we will keep our commitment to poor children who need help with their reading. I know that your foundation has long had a special interest in literacy.

I will be calling you next week to see if such a conference might be scheduled.

We know that the Harkins Foundation has long supported ventures such as ours. We hope we can join those school systems that have received funding for proposals that made a difference.

- Special funding areas

- Proposal deadlines and requirements.

Use that computer document to maintain a record of your contacts, like this example:

2/23. Called Walker of the Harkins Foundation to arrange for a preliminary conference. Will visit her office on 3/1.

Make Personal Contact

The next step is to make personal contact with one of the funding staff. Many successful proposal writers say that this personal contact makes a big difference for both parties. You can get some very useful advice, and the funding staff can size you up face-to-face. Either call first or write an inquiry letter, something similar to the example shown in Box 19.1.

Observe these features in the letter. It begins with a very direct statement of purpose. It provides a brief description of the area served—a subtle way of saying, "We need your help." It shows that the applicant has taken the time to learn about the foundation. Now you are prepared for the phone call and the conference.

Certain guidelines can help you hold a successful conference. First, know as much as you can about the funding agency. Keep the conference focused; you are dealing with important and busy people. Do not smoke, even if invited to do so. Do not make long speeches; let the grantor ask questions if he or she wants more information. Avoid sloganeering and current clichés. Here is an example of what not to say.

> We're interested in developing a new paradigm that will empha- size a holistic approach to systemic reform.

Make it clear that you know where your project wants to go. Indi- cate that you are flexible, but you have a clear sense of purpose. Here is an example of a "money hunter's" lack of purpose that made a very poor impression.

> We're very flexible. We can develop a solid proposal that will meet any of your project emphases. What are you interested in?

Besides knowing the goals of your project, you should also have come prepared with a list of the questions you would like to ask. The following examples show how they might be phrased.

> Could you please tell me a bit more about the foundation's cur- rent interests?
>
> Could you direct me to a successful literacy project that the foun- dation has funded?
>
> Might I read a literacy proposal that you consider excellent?
>
> Are there restrictions on who might apply?
>
> Are there any kinds of activities that the foundation would not support?

Box 19.2   Common Elements of a Proposal

1. Cover letter

2. Title page

3. Abstract

4. Needs to which project will respond

5. Goals and objectives linked with need

6. Project activities

7. Calendar of activities

8. Evaluation of project

9. Applicant capability

10. Budget

Take brief notes, and at the close of the conference, thank the staff member.

WRITING THE PROPOSAL

You should be ready now to write the proposal. Box 19.2 lists the components of a proposal. The components are listed in the order in which they usually occur—and in the order they will be discussed below.

Cover Letter

The cover letter can be very brief, like this one.

Dear Ms. Worey:

We are happy to submit the enclosed proposal, "Reading To-gether." Please feel free to call if you have any questions.

Box 19.3   Title Page

READING TOGETHER:
A PROPOSAL SUBMITTED TO THE
HUNT FOUNDATION

From the United Neighbors of Washington
Contact: Maria Johnson, Box 456
              Washington, NC 27889   October 10, 2003

Title Page

The title page provides some identifying information, as shown in Box 19.3.

Abstract

The abstract is a one-page summary of the project, as shown in Box 19.4. The best way to structure the abstract is to write one or two sentences about each of the topics shown in Box 19.2.

Needs That the Proposal Addresses

Now you should indicate the needs of the project participants. To do so, you carry out a needs assessment and report the results in the proposal. A needs assessment is a systematic study of the special needs of the participants. Each need identified should be supported by evidence, as in the following example.

Parents need to understand how to provide a literate environment in the home in which books are valued, child talk is encouraged, and reading happens. A confidential survey of a sample of 50 parents of students in each grade yielded these results: 82% reported having only one or two books in the residence, parents reported that they spend an average of 15 minutes talking each eve-

---

Box 19.4   Abstract

United Neighbors of Washington (UNW) submits a proposal for funding designed to improve the reading skills of minority students in the Maynard Middle School. Latest state test scores indicate that Maynard ranks in the bottom 10% of all middle schools in the state in reading. In cooperation with the Washington School System, the project staff will take the following actions: recruit and train 15 retired teachers, identify 15 students needing the greatest help in reading, recruit and train the parents, and present 15 Reading Together sessions using reading triads. To encourage parent participation, child care services will be provided. Both formative and summative evaluations will be conducted. In the formative evaluation, all participants will complete a Likert-type evaluation form at the completion of each session. Summative evaluation will employ the Allen Reading Test at both the beginning and the end of the project. A sum of $75,000 is requested.

---

ning with their children, and 45% indicated that they would like to attend instruction/discussion sessions at the school.

Goals and Objectives of the Project

The project goals are the overall outcomes you wish to achieve. Ordinarily, a project will have one or two goals, each of which can be stated in one sentence, as this example shows.

The goals of this project are to improve the reading ability of middle school minority youth and to enable parents to provide a literate environment.

The objectives are the specific outcomes that make up the goal. Usually, you would identify three to five outcomes for each goal. The reading goal might have these objectives:

Box 19.5   Activities Linked With Objectives

Parents will learn how to provide a literate environment.

1. The triads will meet for all sessions in the neighborhood church, from 7-8:30 p.m. for four sessions. Refreshments will be available.

2. Workshop leader will use the ideas of participants to identify these key elements of a literate environment: family discussing books and community happenings, family keeping a reading journal, family talking about new words, and family building its own library. Each family will receive a sum of $50 from the project budget.

3. Participants will view and discuss a videotape of a woman from the community who provides such an environment despite a low income.

---

1. Participating students will significantly improve in word recognition skills.

2. Students will improve in their reading comprehension skills.

3. Students will read an average of three books during the life of the project.

4. Parents will learn how to provide a literate environment.

Project Activities

The project activities are the actions you will take to achieve the objectives. Connect the activities directly with the objectives; do not simply list them at random. You may find it useful to show the relationship directly, in the manner illustrated in Box 19.5. Be sure that all activities are professionally sound and focused on objectives.

Calendar of Activities

You will usually be asked to include a calendar of activities. You have three choices here. First, you may organize the calendar by listing the tentative dates of each activity, like this:

Hold first training activity. May 15.

Second, you may list the activities in chronological order, like this:

March 10. Identify students.

March 14. Recruit parents.

Finally, you may construct a modified Grant chart, similar to the one shown in Box 19.6. Across the top of the chart, you list the time periods—weeks for a shorter project, months for a longer one. Down the left side, you list the categories of activities. Then you show the activities for each category. The chief advantage of the chart is that it shows clearly the interconnection of activities. Thus, if you show a key activity of "Hold first session," you are reminded to enter an "evaluation" in the same month.

Evaluation of the Project

Most funding agencies will want you to explain how you will evaluate the project. Project evaluation is ordinarily reported as *formative* and *summative*. Formative evaluation is what you do to evaluate while the project is under way. Here are some ways you can get formative data for a workshop you wish to evaluate.

- *Observation.* Observe the trainer for presentation skills; observe the participants for signs of inattention.

- *Survey.* Survey participants for their perceptions of the value of the session.

- *Interview.* Hold brief interviews with five participants chosen at random.

- *Document analysis.* Evaluate handouts.

Box 19.6 Modified Grant Chart: Calendar

Area/Month	March	April	May	June
Project Administration	Identify students, teachers; recruit parents	Place book orders; meet with principal		
Training	Plan workshop		Hold 1st session	Hold 2nd and 3rd sessions
Curriculum	Review knowledge base			
Communication		Orient faculty	Publish first article	
Evaluation	Have consultant review plans		Evaluate first workshop	

The main purpose of formative evaluation is to get current data in order to make mid-course corrections.

A summative evaluation is conducted at the close of the project to assess its impact. One simple way to plan a summative evaluation is to show how you will assess the effectiveness of each objective, as in this example:

Students will read an average of three books during the life of the project.

1. Students will keep a reading log.

2. Students will report briefly to the class on books read.

3. Parents will be interviewed.

Applicant Capability

A funding agency wants to know, "Can these people pull off a project this size?" Applicant capability gives you a chance to convince the agency that your organization is capable of succeeding. Here is how that section might sound.

This applicant is fully capable of carrying out the project successfully if funded. We have a track record of success. In the past 3 years, we have had three grants totaling $245,000—the last of which was totally funded by your foundation. And each grant has supported a highly successful project. We have effective leadership. Juan Manoza, retired educator and well-known community activist, has agreed to direct the project; his resumé is attached. He will direct a project faculty of retired reading teachers, all of whom have been identified and evaluated. The local school system has agreed to share up-to-date technology and facilities, as required.

Budget

Most funding agencies have their own budget forms and directions for completing them. In addition to completing the form accurately, keep these guidelines in mind. First, keep the indirect costs as low as possible. The indirect cost is the budget amount paid to the sponsoring organization for its hidden costs in supporting the project. For example, one university charges 40% of the project budget for administrative or indirect costs, such as the costs of providing a library, cooling the classrooms, and maintaining the facility. Funding agencies seem suspicious of indirect costs more than 20%; some government agencies are not allowed to fund any indirect costs.

Second, show some cost sharing by your own agency. You can assume all indirect costs, use the members of your organization as volunteer consultants, bundle a small grant with a larger one, or have your organization make a direct contribution.

Finally, reduce the "hardware" request. Funding agencies are critical of budgets that want funds for video cameras, office furniture, and the like.

RESOURCES

Most of the resources listed below should be available in a large university or community library. Note that most of the publications are also available online.

Organization

The Grantsmanship Center, 1125 West 6th Street, 5th Floor, P.O. Box 17220, Los Angeles, CA 90017

Publications

Federal Register. Superintendent of Documents, U.S. Government Printing Office, Washington DC, 20402

Foundation Directory. 750 Third Avenue, New York, NY 10003

Fund Raiser's Guide to Human Service Funding (current edition). The Taft Group, 5130 MacArthur Blvd. NW, Washington, DC 20016.

PART VI

Conclusion

CHAPTER TWENTY

A Look Behind and a Look Ahead

This is not the usual summary, which simply rehashes what the author has already said. Instead, this chapter takes a retrospective view about what really matters, and then it takes a look ahead about the articles and books you will write.

A LOOK BEHIND

The preceding chapters have included a great deal of information. That information will probably make more sense if you can remember and apply six big ideas that bring together the separate recommendations.

1. *Become a published writing professional.* You need to learn some skills and acquire some information—the province of this work. More importantly, you need to develop some habits of mind: reflecting and finding meaning in your experience; taking a risk by submitting your article or book to an editor's critical eye; and developing a thick skin, through accepting and profiting from criticism.

2. *Think synergistically.* Make long-term plans that enable you to space out your work, taking into consideration the pressures of work, family, writing, and career development. Write an article that can become the basis of a book. Write a book that will advance your career.

3. *Write about what you know.* That recommendation implies taking two related journeys. First, reflect about your experiential knowledge—what you have learned by being in schools. Plumb the depths to find patterns of meaning. Second, broaden your empirical knowledge by accessing and searching useful databases. The two kinds of knowledge complement each other.

4. *Use the writing process flexibly.* This work has presented these components of the writing process: finding a topic, building the knowledge base, organizing your writing, writing the first draft, editing and revising, and working with editors and publishers. Juggle those processes in any way that results in good professional writing.

5. *Know your audience and write to and for it.* One of the best ways to get to know your audience members is to read journals written for them, analyzing such issues as preferred length of article, amount of research cited, formality of style, and common organizational patterns.

6. *Analyze the medium.* This book has presented specific recommendations for the following types: practitioner journal, research journal, opinion piece, the big book, the Internet, the literature review, the research proposal, the master's thesis, the dissertation, an article for the local paper, and the funding proposal.

A Look Ahead

So, where do you go from here? Begin to write an article during the next weekend available to you. Stop talking about writing. Write. There is no substitute for writing. Ask a trusted colleague to review the article for you—not your spouse, not your boss, not your best friend.

Review the feedback, and profit from what your colleague has suggested. Revise the article accordingly—on the first weekend available after receiving the feedback. Mail the article to the journal for which you have written.

If you get a rejection letter, post it on your bulletin board. Grit your teeth, and go through the writing process again.

Index

CORWIN
PRESS

The Corwin Press logo—a raven striding across an open book—represents the happy union of courage and learning. We are a professional-level publisher of books and journals for K–12 educators, and we are committed to creating and providing resources that embody these qualities. Corwin's motto is "Success for All Learners."